GASTRIC SLEEVE BARIATRIC COOKBOOK

1200 Days Of Effortless And Delicious Recipes

To Maintain Your Weight Loss And Nourish Your New Stomach.

Embrace A Healthier Lifestyle Without Compromising On Flavor

BY ROBERT K. EDWARDS

Copyright Robert K. Edwards 2024

- All rights reserved -

Reproduction, duplication, or transmission of the content of this book is strictly prohibited without the written authorization of the author or the publisher.

In no event shall the publisher or the author be liable for any damages, compensations, or monetary losses arising from the information contained in this book, whether directly or indirectly. You are responsible for your own choices, actions, and outcomes.

Disclaimer Notice

Please note that the information contained in this document is for educational and entertainment purposes only. Every effort has been made to present accurate, up-to-date, reliable, and complete information. No warranties of any kind, whether expressed or implied, are provided. Readers acknowledge that the author does not intend to provide legal, financial, medical, or professional advice. The content of this book is sourced from various references.

It is recommended to consult with a licensed professional before attempting to apply the techniques described in this book.

By reading this document, the reader agrees that under no circumstances shall the author be liable for any loss, direct or indirect, incurred as a result of using the information contained herein, including but not limited to errors, omissions, or inaccuracies.

INTRODUCTION ……………… 9

1. INTRODUCTION TO GASTRIC SLEEVE BARIATRIC SURGERY ……………… 11

2. THE SURGICAL PROCESS: WHAT TO EXPECT ……………… 15

3. EMBRACING A NEW LIFESTYLE ……………… 21

4. UNDERSTANDING NUTRITIONAL NEEDS ……………… 24

5. UNDERSTANDING COMMON CHALLENGES ……………… 27

6. UNDERSTANDING COMMON CHALLENGES ……………… 30

7. EMBRACING YOUR NEW LIFE WITH GASTRIC SLEEVE SURGERY ……………… 34

CONCLUSION ……………… 37

REAL STORIES ……………… 38

RECIPES ……………… 44

BREAKFAST ……………… 45

Quinoa Breakfast Bowl ……………… 46

Cottage Cheese Pancakes ……………… 46

Green Protein Smoothie ……………… 47

Avocado Toast ……………… 47

Protein-Packed Breakfast Burrito ……………… 48

Chia Seed Pudding ……………… 48

Protein Pancakes ……………… 49

Berry Protein Smoothie Bowl ……………… 49

LUNCH ……………… 50

Grilled Chicken Salad ……………… 51

Berry Protein Smoothie Bowl ……………… 51

Turkey Lettuce Wraps ……………… 52

Salmon and Quinoa Salad ……………… 52

Caprese Stuffed Chicken Breast ……………… 53

Shrimp and Avocado Salad ……………… 53

Turkey and Vegetable Stir-Fry 54

Greek Chicken Salad 54

Spinach and Feta Stuffed Chicken Breast 55

Tuna Salad Lettuce Wraps 55

Zucchini Noodles with Grilled Chicken 56

Caprese Salad Skewers 56

Mexican Chicken Soup 57

Turkey Lettuce Wrap 57

Quinoa Salad with Grilled Shrimp 58

Egg Salad Lettuce Wraps 58

Greek Chicken Salad 59

Zucchini Noodles with Turkey Meatballs 59

Tuna Avocado Lettuce Wraps 60

Caprese Stuffed Portobello Mushrooms 60

Chicken and Vegetable Stir-Fry 61

Salmon and Asparagus Foil Pack 61

Turkey and Vegetable Lettuce Wraps 62

Quinoa and Black Bean Salad 62

Egg and Vegetable Muffins 63

Spinach and Feta Stuffed Chicken Breast 63

DINNER **64**

Baked Lemon Herb Chicken 65

Zucchini Noodles with Shrimp 65

Turkey Meatballs with Marinara Sauce 66

Grilled Salmon with Asparagus 66

Stuffed Bell Pepper 67

Lemon Herb Baked Chicken 67

Shrimp Stir-Fry with Vegetables 68

Baked Cod with Herbed Quinoa	....	68
Shrimp Stir-Fry with Vegetables	....	69
Baked Cod with Herbed Quinoa	....	69
Grilled Turkey Burger with Sweet Potato Fries	....	70
Baked Eggplant Parmesan	....	70
Grilled Lemon Herb Chicken with Roasted Vegetables	....	71
Baked Cod with Lemon Herb Crust	....	71
Turkey Meatballs with Zucchini Noodles	....	72
Asian-Inspired Beef Stir-Fry	....	72
Stuffed Bell Peppers with Turkey and Quinoa	....	73
Seared Salmon with Quinoa and Steamed Asparagus	....	73
Mexican Chicken Lettuce Wraps	....	74
Veggie Quinoa Bow	....	74

SNACK 75

Greek Yogurt Parfait	....	76
Caprese Skewers	....	76
Deviled Eggs	....	77
Cottage Cheese with Fresh Fruit	....	77
Roasted Chickpeas	....	78
Cottage Cheese with Fresh Fruit	....	78
Turkey Lettuce Wraps	....	79
Tuna Cucumber Bites	....	79
Veggie Egg Muffins	....	80
Apple Slices with Almond Butter	....	80
Protein Shake	....	81
Apple Slices with Almond Butter	....	81

SMOOTHIES 82

- Berry Blast Smoothie 83
- Green Detox Smoothie 83
- Tropical Paradise Smoothie 84
- Green Detox Smoothie 84
- Peanut Butter Banana Smoothie 85
- Creamy Berry Avocado Smoothie 85
- Chocolate Banana Protein Smoothie 86
- Spinach and Mango Smoothie 86
- Raspberry Almond Smoothie 87
- Peach Oatmeal Smoothie 87
- Coconut Pineapple Smoothie 88

SWEET 89

- Berry Chia Pudding 90
- Baked Apples with Cinnamon 90
- Greek Yogurt Parfait 91
- Banana-Oat Cookies 91
- Strawberry Banana Nice Cream 92
- Lemon Poppy Seed Muffins 92
- Cinnamon Apple Crisp 93
- Protein Pancakes 93
- Chocolate Banana Protein Bites 94
- Vanilla Almond Pudding 94
- BONUS 1: HIIT 96
- BONUS 2: 4-WEEK MEAL PLAN 97
- BONUS 3: WEIGHT LOSS JOURNAL 98
- BONUS 4: THE LOW-FODMAP DIET COOKBOOK 99

INTRODUCTION

In a world where obesity is running rampant and health risks are lurking around every corner, finding effective weight management strategies is no small feat. But fear not! Enter bariatric surgery, the superhero of the weight loss world, here to rescue you from the clutches of severe obesity and transform your life for the better.

Picture this: **GASTRIC SLEEVE BARIATRIC COOKBOOK** is the ultimate must-have book for all you brave souls embarking on or already knee-deep in the bariatric surgery journey. Think of it as your trusty sidekick, packed to the brim with mind-blowing knowledge, practical tips to help you make smart decisions about your health, and an array of mouthwatering recipes specifically tailored for your post-surgery palate. This book is on a mission to demystify bariatric surgery, showering you with a deep understanding of the entire process, its glorious benefits, and the inevitable challenges that lie ahead. It's your secret weapon, equipping you both mentally and physically to conquer the rollercoaster ride of surgery and embrace the necessary changes for long-term success.

But wait, there's more! This book isn't just about the nitty-gritty details of the surgery itself. It's an all-inclusive package, guiding you from pre-op prep to post-op paradise. It's your go-to megastore for all the crucial stuff like what to devour, how to bust a move, how to kickstart your motivation, and where to find the support crew you deserve. We're talking a dream team of experts, from doctors and dieticians to therapists and support groups, all rallying behind your triumphant transformation. And hey, this book isn't some dull clinical manual. It's brimming with real stories from fellow bariatric warriors, reminding you that you're never alone in this battle. It digs deep into the emotional trenches, addressing body image woes and self-esteem struggles like a trusted confidant, guiding you through the darkest of times.

But hold onto your hats, because we've got a jaw-dropping surprise in store for you: **GASTRIC SLEEVE BARIATRIC COOKBOOK** isn't just a guidebook—it's a bona fide culinary extravaganza! That's right, folks, prepare to have your taste buds waltz through a gastronomic wonderland. Packed with lip-smacking recipes specifically tailored for the bariatric-savvy, this book has got your post-surgery dining covered. Say goodbye to dull meals and hello to breakfasts that will have your taste buds twerking, main courses that will make you weak in the knees, and desserts that will leave you guilt-free and grinning from ear to ear. And these recipes aren't some haphazard concoctions; oh no, they're crafted with love to give your body the nutrients it craves. We're talking lean proteins, wholesome grains, fiber-packed veggies, and the kind of fats that won't send you running for the hills. And here's the kicker—they're not just healthy, they're downright delicious! We've got options for the veggie lovers, gluten-free gang, and anyone with a taste for the extraordinary. Each recipe comes with crystal-clear instructions, so even if you're not Gordon Ramsay in the kitchen, you'll be whipping up masterpieces in no time. Plus, the book spills the beans on meal planning, ingredient swapping, and recipe customization, making it a breeze to cater to your unique preferences. And did we mention it breaks down all the nutritional info too? Say hello to keeping tabs on calories, carbs, protein, and fat, all while tantalizing your taste buds.

By combining the wisdom and guidance of a bariatric surgery guru with the mouthwatering delights of a culinary genius, this book is a force to be reckoned with. It's a one-of-a-kind, priceless resource for those eager to embrace a healthier lifestyle post-bariatric surgery. It arms you with the knowledge, inspiration, and practical tools needed to navigate the treacherous waters of weight loss, improve your overall well-being, and embark on a culinary journey like no other. So grab a copy, buckle up, and get ready to conquer the world—one delicious recipe at a time.

1. INTRODUCTION TO GASTRIC SLEEVE BARIATRIC SURGERY

1.1 Understanding Obesity and its Impact on Health

Millions of individuals from various ages and socioeconomic backgrounds are affected by obesity, which has emerged as a major global health issue. It is a serious condition with considerable dangers to both physical and mental health that is defined by an excessive buildup of body fat. It's critical to first realize the effects of obesity on health in order to fully appreciate the significance of gastric sleeve bariatric surgery. The body mass index (BMI), which computes the ratio of a person's weight to height, is commonly used to assess obesity. BMI ranges are used to categorize obesity, with a BMI of 30 or more being considered obese. However, it is important to note that BMI is just one indicator and may not account for factors such as muscle mass or individual variations.

The prevalence of obesity has reached alarming levels globally, leading to serious health implications. Individuals with obesity are at a higher risk of developing various chronic conditions, including cardiovascular disease, type 2 diabetes, hypertension, stroke, certain types of cancer, and joint problems. These health risks can significantly impact a person's quality of life, leading to decreased mobility, increased pain, and a higher likelihood of mental health disorders such as depression and anxiety.

1.2 Overview of Bariatric Surgery Options

Bariatric surgery has emerged as a bona fide game-changer, proving its mettle in the realm of weight loss and transforming the health outcomes of individuals grappling with obesity. Within this realm, different bariatric procedures hold their own unique advantages and considerations. Enter gastric sleeve bariatric surgery, a marvel also known as sleeve gastrectomy. This procedure works its magic by bidding adieu to a substantial portion of the stomach, fashioning a smaller, banana-shaped pouch in its wake. Rest assured, this surgical masterpiece takes a primarily restrictive approach, curbing the stomach's capacity and reining in the amount of food that can be savored in a single sitting. But that's not all—

gastric sleeve surgery boasts metabolic perks too, triggering hormonal changes that regulate the appetite and set the stage for impressive weight loss.

Now, let's embark on a journey of comparison, shall we? When sizing up different bariatric procedures, gastric sleeve surgery emerges as a true victor, draped in a cloak of undeniable advantages. Firstly, it treads lightly when it comes to nutritional deficiencies, unlike its malabsorptive counterparts like gastric bypass. You see, gastric sleeve surgery allows the intestines to maintain their integrity, sidestepping the hurdles of nutritional inadequacies. Furthermore, this surgical wonder eliminates the need for external devices like the adjustable gastric band, sparing individuals the hassle of ongoing adjustments and sparingly low long-term success rates. And if that weren't enough, gastric sleeve surgery dazzles with its triumphant track record in weight loss and the amelioration of obesity-related companions such as diabetes and hypertension.

In a nutshell, gastric sleeve bariatric surgery stands tall as a formidable contender, armed with its repertoire of benefits and achievements. It reshapes lives, transforms health, and presents a beacon of hope for individuals seeking a profound and lasting change.

1.3 Benefits and Considerations of Gastric Sleeve Surgery

Individuals battling with obesity can benefit from gastric sleeve surgery in a variety of ways. The primary benefit is dramatic weight loss, with studies indicating that patients can lose 50-70% of their excess body weight within the first year of operation. This weight loss not only improves physical appearance but also has a significant impact on general health and well-being. Gastric sleeve surgery causes metabolic alterations and hormonal modulation in addition to weight loss. The surgery removes a portion of the stomach responsible for producing ghrelin, a hormone that stimulates hunger. As a result, patients often experience a reduced appetite and improved control over food cravings, leading to sustained weight loss. The metabolic changes associated with gastric sleeve surgery also contribute to the improvement or resolution of obesity-related conditions, such as type 2 diabetes and high blood pressure. While gastric sleeve surgery offers numerous benefits, it is essential to consider certain factors before making a decision. First and foremost, gastric sleeve surgery is not a quick fix or a standalone solution for weight loss. It requires a lifelong commitment to dietary and lifestyle modifications to ensure long-term success. Patients must adopt healthier eating habits, portion control, and regular physical activity to maintain their weight loss and prevent weight regain.

Another consideration is the potential for complications and risks associated with any surgical procedure. Although gastric sleeve surgery is generally safe, it is not without risks. Possible complications include infection, bleeding, leaks, and strictures. However, the risk of complications can be minimized by selecting an experienced surgeon and following the recommended post-operative care.

1.4 Preparing Physically and Mentally for the Procedure

Before undergoing gastric sleeve surgery, individuals need to engage in comprehensive pre-operative preparation to optimize their surgical outcomes and ensure a smoother recovery. This preparation includes various physical and mental aspects.

Physically, patients will undergo a series of evaluations and tests to assess their overall health and determine if they are suitable candidates for surgery. Medical assessments may include blood tests, imaging studies, and consultations with specialists to rule out any underlying conditions that may affect the surgery. Additionally, patients may undergo a psychological evaluation to assess their readiness for the emotional and psychological changes that accompany the surgery.

Nutritional counseling is a vital component of pre-operative preparation. Patients will receive guidance from registered dietitians on making dietary changes that promote weight loss and improve overall health. These changes may involve reducing calorie intake, increasing protein consumption, and incorporating nutrient-dense foods into their diet. Patients may also be advised to follow a pre-operative diet to shrink the liver and reduce surgical risks.

In addition to physical preparation, mental and emotional readiness is crucial for a successful surgical journey. Patients must understand the potential challenges and lifestyle modifications required after surgery. This includes adjusting their relationship with food, developing coping strategies for emotional eating, and establishing a support system that includes family, friends, and healthcare professionals. Having a strong support network can help individuals navigate the physical and emotional changes associated with the surgery and ensure a more positive outcome.

1.5 Setting Realistic Expectations and Goals

When considering gastric sleeve surgery, it is essential for individuals to set realistic expectations and goals. While weight loss is a primary goal, it is crucial to understand that the surgery is a tool and not a guarantee for instant and effortless weight loss. It requires a commitment to long-term lifestyle changes and adherence to post-operative guidelines.

Weight loss following gastric sleeve surgery typically occurs gradually over a period of 12-18 months. The initial weeks after surgery may show rapid weight loss due to a significant reduction in calorie intake. However, weight loss tends to stabilize over time, and patients should expect a slower rate of weight loss in the long term. Setting realistic goals based on an individual's unique circumstances and consulting with healthcare professionals can help manage expectations and ensure a more sustainable weight loss journey.

In addition to weight loss, individuals can expect improvements in obesity-related comorbidities such as type 2 diabetes, high blood pressure, and sleep apnea. However, the extent of improvement may vary from person to person, and some comorbidities may not completely resolve. It is important to understand that surgery does not eliminate all health risks associated with obesity, and ongoing medical management and follow-up are still necessary. Furthermore, gastric sleeve surgery is not a cure-all solution for emotional or psychological struggles related to food. While the surgery can provide a fresh start and an opportunity to develop healthier habits, it is essential to address the underlying psychological factors contributing to overeating or emotional eating. This may involve seeking therapy, attending support groups, or working with a mental health professional to develop coping mechanisms and address any emotional challenges. By setting realistic expectations and goals, individuals can approach gastric sleeve surgery with a clear understanding of what to expect and a commitment to the necessary lifestyle changes. This mindset is crucial for long-term success and ensures that individuals are mentally prepared to embrace the physical and emotional transformations that accompany the surgical journey.

In this chapter, we provided a comprehensive overview of obesity, the impact of obesity on health, different bariatric surgery options, the benefits and considerations of gastric sleeve surgery, pre-operative preparation, and setting realistic expectations and goals. By understanding these fundamental aspects, individuals can make informed decisions about their weight loss journey and embark on a path towards improved health and well-being.

2. THE SURGICAL PROCESS: WHAT TO EXPECT

2.1 Preparing for Surgery: Consultations and Evaluations

Before undergoing gastric sleeve surgery, individuals will go through a series of consultations and evaluations to ensure they are physically and mentally prepared for the procedure. This chapter explores the various steps involved in preparing for surgery and what patients can expect during this phase.

The pre-operative phase of bariatric surgery involves a comprehensive process of evaluations and consultations to ensure that patients are prepared physically, nutritionally, and psychologically for the procedure. These assessments are essential in identifying any underlying medical conditions and assessing the patient's readiness for the surgery. During the pre-operative consultations, patients meet with their surgical team, including the surgeon, anesthesiologist, and other healthcare professionals involved in their care. These consultations serve as an opportunity for patients to discuss their concerns, ask questions, and gain a thorough understanding of the surgical process. The healthcare professionals provide detailed information about the procedure, including its benefits, potential risks, and expected outcomes.

Medical assessments are conducted to evaluate the patient's overall health and fitness for surgery. This may include blood tests to assess various parameters such as blood count, liver function, and kidney function. Imaging studies, such as X-rays or ultrasounds, may be performed to assess the patient's anatomy and identify any abnormalities that could impact the surgical process. Additionally, an electrocardiogram (ECG) may be done to evaluate the patient's heart health and ensure that they can safely undergo anesthesia and surgery.

Nutritional assessment and counseling play a vital role in the pre-operative phase. Patients meet with a registered dietitian who specializes in bariatric surgery to discuss their current eating habits, nutritional needs, and any dietary modifications required before and after surgery. The dietitian provides guidance on adopting a pre-operative diet aimed at reducing the size of the liver, which can facilitate the surgical procedure and minimize complications. This may involve limiting calorie intake, reducing carbohydrates, and increasing protein consumption. The dietitian also educates patients on post-operative dietary guidelines, including portion sizes, nutrient requirements, and recommended food choices to support optimal healing and long-term weight loss.

In addition to the physical evaluations, a psychological evaluation is typically conducted to assess the patient's readiness for gastric sleeve surgery. This evaluation helps identify any psychological factors that may impact the patient's ability to adhere to the necessary lifestyle changes and cope with the emotional aspects of the surgical process. A mental health professional, such as a psychologist or psychiatrist, will evaluate the patient's emotional well-being, assess their understanding of the surgery, and explore any history of mental health conditions or disordered eating patterns. This evaluation is essential to ensure that patients have realistic expectations, a strong support system in place, and the necessary coping skills to navigate the physical and emotional changes associated with the surgery. Overall, the pre-operative phase of bariatric surgery is a comprehensive and thorough process designed to evaluate and prepare patients for the life-changing procedure. Through medical assessments, nutritional counseling, and psychological evaluations, the healthcare team ensures that patients are physically and mentally prepared, setting the stage for a successful surgical journey and long-term weight loss success.

2.2 The Day of Surgery: Preparing for the Procedure

Summary:

The pre-operative phase of gastric sleeve surgery involves several consultations and assessments to ensure the patient's readiness for the procedure. These consultations include discussions with the surgical team, such as the surgeon, anesthesiologist, and other healthcare professionals involved in the patient's care. The purpose is to address any concerns, provide information about the surgical process, and evaluate the patient's overall health.

Medical assessments, such as blood tests, imaging studies, and electrocardiograms, are conducted to identify any underlying medical conditions that may impact the surgical process. These assessments ensure that the patient is in optimal health for the procedure.

Nutritional assessment and counseling play a crucial role in the pre-operative phase. Patients meet with a registered dietitian specializing in bariatric surgery to discuss their current eating habits, nutritional needs, and necessary dietary modifications. A pre-operative diet is often recommended to reduce the size of the liver, improving surgical outcomes. This may involve calorie restriction, reducing carbohydrates, and increasing protein intake. The dietitian also educates patients about post-operative dietary guidelines, including portion sizes, nutrient requirements, and food choices.

In addition to physical evaluations, a psychological evaluation is typically conducted to assess the patient's readiness for gastric sleeve surgery. This evaluation aims to identify any psychological factors that may impact adherence to lifestyle changes and emotional well-being during the surgical process. A mental health professional assesses the patient's emotional state, understanding of the surgery, and any history of mental health conditions or disordered eating patterns. This evaluation ensures that patients have realistic expectations, a strong support system, and the necessary coping skills for the physical and emotional changes associated with the surgery.

By delving deeper into the pre-operative phase, patients gain a comprehensive understanding of the consultations, medical assessments, and evaluations that contribute to their overall readiness for gastric sleeve surgery. This ensures that they are physically and mentally prepared for the procedure and have the necessary support systems in place for a successful surgical journey.

Following the completion of the surgical procedure, patients will be moved to the recovery area, where they will be closely monitored by the healthcare team. This section will provide detailed information on the immediate postoperative care, including pain management, the use of drains if necessary, and the transition from the recovery area to the hospital room.

Patients will be instructed on postoperative mobility, breathing exercises, and the use of compression stockings to reduce the risk of blood clots. They will also receive guidance on the progression of the diet and the importance of regular follow-up appointments to monitor progress and address any concerns.

2.3 Potential Risks and Complications

While gastric sleeve surgery is generally considered safe, it is essential to be aware of the potential risks and complications associated with the procedure. This section provides an in-depth discussion of these risks, emphasizing the importance of informed consent and the role of the healthcare team in mitigating and managing these risks.

2.3.1 Surgical Risks

Surgical risks include but are not limited to infection, bleeding, blood clots, anesthesia complications, injury to surrounding organs, and adverse reactions to medications. The chapter will explore these risks, their likelihood, and the steps taken by the surgical team to minimize them.

Postoperative complications may include leaks along the staple line, strictures (narrowing of the stomach opening), gastrointestinal obstruction, dumping syndrome (rapid emptying of food into the small intestine), and nutritional deficiencies. This section will discuss the signs, symptoms, and management of these complications.

2.4 Psychological Preparation for Surgery

Undergoing gastric sleeve surgery involves not only physical changes but also emotional and psychological adjustments. This section addresses the importance of psychological preparation, including discussions with a mental health professional, support networks, and coping strategies to navigate the challenges and emotional aspects associated with the surgery.

Successful gastric sleeve surgery relies on the expertise and collaboration of a multidisciplinary surgical team. This section explores the roles of different healthcare professionals involved in the surgical process, including the surgeon, anesthesiologist, nurses, dietitians, and psychologists. Readers will gain insight into how each member contributes to the overall care and support provided to patients before, during, and after surgery.

2.5 Frequently Asked Questions (FAQs)

To address common concerns and queries, this section provides a comprehensive list of frequently asked questions related to the surgical process. It covers topics such as anesthesia safety, recovery time, scarring, postoperative pain management, and the impact of the surgery on fertility and pregnancy.

By addressing these FAQs, readers will have access to the information they need to make informed decisions and alleviate any apprehensions they may have.

Q: Is bariatric surgery a good option for me?

A: Bariatric surgery is a viable option for individuals struggling with severe obesity and its associated health risks. However, it is important to consult with a healthcare professional to determine if you are a suitable candidate based on your overall health, medical history, and weight loss goals.

Q: What are the different types of bariatric surgeries available?

A: There are several types of bariatric surgeries, including gastric bypass, gastric sleeve, and gastric banding. Gastric bypass involves rerouting the digestive system, while gastric sleeve involves removing a portion of the stomach. Gastric banding involves placing an adjustable band around the stomach. Each procedure has its own benefits and considerations, and the best option for you will depend on various factors discussed with your healthcare provider.

Q: How long does the recovery process take after bariatric surgery?

A: The recovery period can vary for each individual, but typically, patients spend a few days in the hospital after the surgery. You may experience discomfort and need to follow a liquid or soft diet initially. Over time, you will gradually transition to regular solid foods. It is important to follow your healthcare provider's instructions and attend follow-up appointments for monitoring your progress.

Q: Will I be able to eat normal meals after bariatric surgery?

A: Bariatric surgery does bring changes to your eating habits. Initially, your portions will be smaller, and you'll need to focus on nutrient-dense foods. Over time, as your body adjusts, you will be able to enjoy a wide variety of foods, but in smaller quantities. It is crucial to adopt a balanced and healthy diet to support your weight loss and overall well-being.

Q: Will I need to take supplements after bariatric surgery?

A: Yes, after bariatric surgery, your body's ability to absorb certain nutrients may be affected. You will likely need to take supplements, such as multivitamins, calcium, iron, and vitamin B12, to ensure you are meeting your nutritional needs. It is essential to follow your healthcare provider's guidance and have regular blood tests to monitor your nutrient levels.

Q: How long does it take to see significant weight loss after bariatric surgery?

A: Weight loss after bariatric surgery varies among individuals. In the first few months following the surgery, you can expect to lose a significant amount of weight. However, the rate of weight loss may slow down over time. It is important to remember that bariatric surgery is a tool to support weight loss, and your commitment to adopting a healthy lifestyle, including regular exercise and a balanced diet, plays a vital role in achieving long-term success.

Note: It's important to consult with a healthcare professional for personalized advice regarding bariatric surgery and its implications. The answers provided here are for informational purposes only and should not replace professional medical guidance.

Note: The subsequent chapters will continue to delve into other crucial aspects of gastric sleeve bariatric surgery, including preoperative and postoperative nutrition, lifestyle changes, long-term follow-up, and specific cooking recipes tailored for patients who have undergone gastric surgery.

3. EMBRACING A NEW LIFESTYLE

After undergoing gastric sleeve surgery, embracing a new lifestyle becomes paramount for long-term success. This section delves into the fundamental changes that individuals must make to adjust to their post-surgery life.

a) Adopting a Healthier Diet: adopting a healthier diet is crucial for maintaining overall health and well-being. By choosing nutrient-rich foods and minimizing the consumption of processed and unhealthy options, we provide our bodies with the necessary fuel to thrive. A healthy diet, rich in fruits, vegetables, whole grains, lean proteins, and healthy fats, supports optimal bodily functions, boosts the immune system, and reduces the risk of chronic diseases. Transitioning to a healthier diet requires prioritizing whole foods, practicing portion control, and staying hydrated. It is a long-term commitment that brings numerous benefits, including weight management, increased energy levels, improved digestion, enhanced cognitive function, and a higher quality of life. By embracing a healthier diet, we can nourish our bodies, prioritize our health, and pave the way for a vibrant and fulfilling life.

b) Developing an Exercise Routine: Regular physical activity is essential for maintaining weight loss and improving overall health. This section guides readers on how to gradually incorporate exercise into their daily routine, considering their physical capabilities and any limitations following surgery. It will cover various exercise options, including cardiovascular activities, strength training, and flexibility exercises, while emphasizing the importance of consistency and finding activities that are enjoyable and sustainable.

c) Managing Portion Sizes: Portion control plays a crucial role in maintaining weight loss after gastric sleeve surgery. This segment will provide practical strategies for gauging appropriate portion sizes and managing hunger and satiety cues. Readers will learn about mindful eating techniques, the importance of eating slowly and chewing thoroughly, and utilizing smaller plates and utensils to create a visual illusion of larger portions.

d) Establishing a Regular Eating Schedule: Developing a consistent eating schedule is vital to maintain a balanced metabolism and promote healthy digestion. This section will delve into the significance of establishing regular meal and snack times and spacing them appropriately throughout the day. Readers will gain insights into creating a structured eating routine that accommodates their individual needs and supports sustainable weight loss.

3.1 Navigating Emotional and Psychological Changes

Undergoing weight loss surgery brings about significant emotional and psychological changes. This section delves into the psychological aspects of the post-surgery journey, helping readers navigate and address these changes effectively.

a) Body Image Concerns: Weight loss can alter an individual's body shape and size, which may impact their body image and self-esteem. This segment will provide guidance on developing a positive body image and coping with any challenges that arise. Strategies may include practicing self-acceptance, seeking professional counseling or therapy, and connecting with support groups where individuals can share their experiences and gain insights from others who have undergone similar transformations.

b) Adjusting to a New Self-Perception: After weight loss surgery, individuals may need time to adjust to their new self-perception and identity. This section will explore the emotional aspects of self-image and guide readers in developing a positive and realistic sense of self. It may cover topics such as setting realistic expectations, embracing personal growth beyond physical changes, and cultivating self-compassion throughout the journey.

c) Managing Emotional Eating Tendencies: Emotional eating can be a significant challenge for many individuals both before and after surgery. This segment will delve into strategies for identifying emotional triggers and developing alternative coping mechanisms to food. Readers will learn about stress management techniques, practicing mindful eating, and seeking support from mental health professionals to address emotional eating tendencies effectively.

d) Seeking Support: Building a strong support system is crucial during the post-surgery phase. This section emphasizes the importance of seeking support from healthcare professionals, support groups, and loved ones. Readers will learn how to communicate their needs effectively, engage in open and honest conversations with their support network, and seek professional guidance when needed.

Additionally, online communities and resources that provide a platform for individuals to connect and share their experiences may be highlighted.

3.2 Establishing a Nutritional Plan

Maintaining proper nutrition is vital after gastric sleeve surgery to support overall health and prevent nutrient deficiencies. This section focuses on establishing a well-rounded nutritional plan that meets the specific needs of individuals post-surgery.

a) Meeting Nutritional Requirements: Readers will gain an understanding of the essential nutrients their bodies require and how to meet these requirements through a balanced diet. This may include information on macronutrients (carbohydrates, proteins, and fats) and micronutrients (vitamins and minerals) and their roles in supporting overall health. Tips for selecting nutrient-dense foods and considering dietary supplements, as recommended by healthcare professionals, may also be provided.

b) Hydration: Staying adequately hydrated is crucial for optimal health and digestion. This segment emphasizes the importance of consuming an adequate amount of fluids daily and provides tips on maintaining hydration levels post-surgery. Readers will learn about the recommended fluid intake, strategies for tracking and monitoring hydration, and identifying signs of dehydration.

c) Managing Digestive Changes: Gastric sleeve surgery alters the digestive process, and individuals must adapt to these changes. This section explores common digestive changes post-surgery, such as reduced stomach capacity and changes in nutrient absorption. Practical advice on managing digestive symptoms, such as dumping syndrome or indigestion, may be provided. Readers will gain insights into eating strategies, including chewing thoroughly, avoiding certain foods that may cause discomfort, and prioritizing nutrient-dense options.

d) Long-Term Follow-Up and Monitoring: Long-term follow-up care is essential for individuals who have undergone gastric sleeve surgery. This segment emphasizes the importance of regular check-ups with healthcare professionals, including dietitians and surgeons, to monitor progress, address any concerns, and ensure ongoing support. Readers will gain an understanding of the follow-up schedule and the significance of ongoing monitoring to maintain their health and well-being.

4. UNDERSTANDING NUTRITIONAL NEEDS

In this section, readers will gain a comprehensive understanding of the nutritional needs specific to individuals who have undergone gastric sleeve surgery. It will cover the key nutrients required for overall health, weight management, and prevention of nutrient deficiencies.

a) Macronutrients: Readers will learn about the importance of macronutrients, including carbohydrates, proteins, and fats, in their post-surgery diet. They will understand how to balance these macronutrients to support weight loss, provide energy, and promote muscle health. Practical tips on choosing nutrient-dense carbohydrates, lean protein sources, and healthy fats will be provided.

b) Micronutrients: Micronutrients, such as vitamins and minerals, play a vital role in supporting various bodily functions. This segment will focus on the essential micronutrients that gastric sleeve patients need to pay attention to, including iron, calcium, vitamin B12, vitamin D, and others. Readers will understand the importance of regular monitoring and potential supplementation to prevent nutrient deficiencies.

c) Water-Soluble Fiber: Fiber is an essential component of a healthy diet, aiding digestion and promoting satiety. However, after gastric sleeve surgery, it is crucial to choose fiber sources that are easily digestible. This section will provide guidance on incorporating water-soluble fiber into the diet, including fruits, vegetables, and legumes, to support digestive health without causing discomfort.

4.1 Meal Planning and Portion Control

This section will guide readers on practical meal planning strategies and portion control techniques to ensure they are meeting their nutritional needs while managing their reduced stomach capacity.

a) Balancing Meals: Readers will learn how to create balanced meals that include a variety of food groups and meet their nutritional requirements. This may involve understanding portion sizes for different food groups, such as protein, vegetables, fruits, and grains, and incorporating them into meals effectively.

b) Meal Frequency and Snacking: After gastric sleeve surgery, individuals may need to adjust their meal frequency and approach to snacking. This segment will provide insights into the ideal meal frequency and the importance of spacing meals and snacks appropriately throughout the day. Readers will learn how to make healthy snack choices that contribute to their nutritional goals.

c) Mindful Eating Techniques: Mindful eating is an essential practice for gastric sleeve patients, promoting slower eating, increased awareness of hunger and satiety cues, and better digestion. This section will introduce readers to mindful eating techniques, such as savoring each bite, eating without distractions, and listening to their body's signals.

4.2 Strategies for Long-Term Success

Maintaining long-term success after gastric sleeve surgery requires sustainable strategies for healthy eating and lifestyle habits. This section focuses on the practical strategies that readers can implement to support their weight loss goals and overall well-being.

a) Label Reading and Meal Prepping: Understanding food labels and being able to make informed choices is crucial for successful post-surgery nutrition. This segment will provide readers with tips on how to read and interpret food labels effectively. Additionally, meal prepping strategies will be discussed, including planning and preparing meals in advance to ensure access to healthy options throughout the week.

b) Eating Out and Social Situations: Dining out and social events can pose challenges for individuals who have undergone gastric sleeve surgery. This section will provide guidance on navigating these situations, including making smart menu choices, controlling portion sizes, and communicating dietary needs to friends, family, and restaurant staff.

c) Coping with Food Cravings and Emotional Eating: Dealing with food cravings and emotional eating is a common challenge after surgery. This segment will explore strategies for managing cravings, such as identifying triggers, finding healthier alternatives, and utilizing coping mechanisms that do not involve food.

d) Physical Activity and Exercise: Physical activity plays a crucial role in weight management, overall health, and well-being. This section will discuss the importance of incorporating regular physical activity into the post-surgery routine. Readers will gain insights into appropriate exercises, setting realistic goals, and finding enjoyable ways to stay active.

5. UNDERSTANDING COMMON CHALLENGES

In this section, readers will gain a comprehensive understanding of the common challenges and plateaus that individuals may encounter on their gastric sleeve surgery journey. By delving deeper into these challenges, readers can develop a strong awareness of potential obstacles and empower themselves to overcome them.

a) Emotional and Psychological Challenges: After undergoing gastric sleeve surgery, individuals often face emotional and psychological challenges that can impact their overall well-being. This segment will explore the various aspects of these challenges, such as body image concerns, self-esteem issues, and emotional eating patterns. Readers will gain insights into the emotional rollercoaster that can accompany significant weight loss, including feelings of joy, frustration, and vulnerability. Understanding the psychological aspects of the journey will enable readers to develop effective coping mechanisms, such as seeking support from loved ones, engaging in therapy or counseling, and practicing self-care strategies.

b) Plateaus and Weight Loss Stalls: Plateaus, periods of stalled weight loss, are common during the gastric sleeve surgery journey. This section will delve into the factors that contribute to plateaus, including metabolic adaptations, changes in body composition, and lifestyle factors. Readers will gain a deeper understanding of why weight loss stalls occur and how they can overcome them. Strategies for breaking through plateaus will be explored, including modifying the dietary approach, incorporating different exercise routines, adjusting macronutrient ratios, and seeking guidance from healthcare professionals. Emphasis will be placed on the importance of patience, perseverance, and trusting the process during these phases.

c) Nutritional Compliance: Maintaining optimal nutrition and adhering to the recommended post-surgery dietary guidelines can pose challenges for individuals. This segment will address the potential difficulties that may arise, such as managing portion sizes, consuming adequate protein, and incorporating nutrient-dense foods. Readers will receive practical tips and strategies to ensure nutritional compliance, including meal planning, prepping healthy meals and snacks, tracking macronutrient intake, and staying hydrated. Additionally, the importance of regular follow-ups with healthcare professionals and support groups will be highlighted to provide ongoing guidance, monitor progress, and address any nutritional concerns.

5.1 Strategies for Overcoming Challenges

This section will equip readers with a range of effective strategies and tools to overcome the challenges and plateaus they may encounter during their gastric sleeve surgery journey. By implementing these strategies, individuals can proactively address obstacles and maintain motivation for long-term success.

a) Goal Setting and Tracking: Setting clear, realistic, and measurable goals is paramount for maintaining focus and tracking progress. This segment will guide readers on how to establish meaningful short-term and long-term goals that align with their individual aspirations. Additionally, readers will learn about different methods of tracking their progress, such as using smartphone apps, food journals, weight logs, and body measurements. Regularly monitoring progress will enable readers to celebrate achievements, identify patterns, and make necessary adjustments to stay motivated on their journey.

b) Behavioral and Lifestyle Modifications: Making sustainable behavioral and lifestyle changes is pivotal for long-term success after gastric sleeve surgery. This section will provide readers with in-depth strategies for adopting healthier habits and addressing underlying factors that contribute to weight gain or hinder progress. Topics covered may include practicing mindful eating, developing portion control skills, managing stress and emotional triggers, improving sleep quality, and incorporating regular physical activity into daily routines. Readers will be encouraged to approach these changes gradually, acknowledging that small, consistent steps yield lasting results.

c) Support Systems and Accountability: Building a robust support system and maintaining accountability are vital during the post-surgery journey. This segment will delve into the various sources of support available, including friends, family, support groups, and healthcare professionals. Readers will gain an understanding of the benefits of joining support groups or seeking individual counseling, where they can share experiences, gain insights, and receive encouragement from others who have undergone similar surgeries. Furthermore, accountability strategies such as finding an accountability partner, participating in online communities, and scheduling regular check-ins with healthcare professionals will be explored.

d) Motivation and Mindset: Sustaining motivation and cultivating a positive mindset are integral to overcoming challenges and plateaus. This section will explore evidence-based techniques to enhance motivation and develop a resilient mindset. Readers will learn about the power of celebrating non-scale victories, setting meaningful rewards, visualizing success, and practicing self-compassion. Additionally, techniques such as positive affirmations, gratitude journaling, meditation, and visualization exercises will be introduced as effective tools to overcome self-doubt, manage stress, and foster a positive outlook throughout the journey.

5.2 Professional Guidance and Support

Seeking professional guidance and support plays a vital role in overcoming challenges and plateaus effectively. This section will emphasize the importance of regular follow-ups with healthcare professionals, nutritionists, and support groups. Readers will gain insights into the valuable role these professionals play in monitoring progress, providing personalized recommendations, and offering guidance tailored to individual needs. The chapter will highlight the significance of scheduling regular appointments, attending support group meetings, and actively engaging in conversations to address concerns, seek clarification, and optimize outcomes. By exploring the common challenges, implementing effective strategies, and seeking professional guidance and support, individuals can navigate the obstacles and plateaus they may encounter after gastric sleeve surgery. This chapter equips readers with the necessary tools, knowledge, and mindset to overcome challenges, maintain motivation, and achieve long-term health and well-being.

6. UNDERSTANDING COMMON CHALLENGES

6.1 The Importance of Sustainable Habits

In this section, readers will understand the significance of adopting sustainable habits to maintain long-term success after gastric sleeve surgery. They will learn that the surgery is a tool for weight loss, but the real transformation lies in making lasting lifestyle changes.

a) Embracing a Healthy Eating Pattern: This segment will delve into the importance of adopting a healthy eating pattern that is sustainable and nourishing. Readers will explore the concept of balanced nutrition, including consuming adequate protein, healthy fats, and nutrient-dense foods. They will learn practical strategies to structure their meals, prioritize whole foods, incorporate fruits and vegetables, and manage portion sizes. Additionally, the chapter will emphasize the value of mindful eating, where individuals learn to listen to their bodies' hunger and fullness cues, savor each bite, and practice gratitude for nourishing their bodies.

b) Staying Active and Engaging in Regular Exercise: Regular physical activity is crucial for maintaining long-term success and overall well-being. This section will provide readers with insights into different types of exercises suitable for their post-surgery journey, including aerobic activities, strength training, and flexibility exercises. Readers will learn about the benefits of exercise, such as improved cardiovascular health, increased energy levels, enhanced mood, and weight maintenance. Strategies for incorporating physical activity into daily routines, overcoming barriers, and staying motivated will be discussed, emphasizing the importance of finding enjoyable activities that fit individual preferences and capabilities.

c) Prioritizing Mental and Emotional Well-being: Mental and emotional well-being are integral components of long-term success. This segment will explore various strategies for managing stress, cultivating resilience, and nurturing positive mental health. Readers will learn about stress management techniques, such as mindfulness meditation, deep breathing exercises, and engaging in activities that promote relaxation and self-care. The chapter will also highlight the importance of seeking professional support if needed, such as therapy or counseling, to address any underlying emotional challenges and develop effective coping mechanisms.

6.2 Navigating Social Situations and Relationships

Maintaining long-term success after gastric sleeve surgery often involves navigating social situations and relationships that can impact lifestyle choices and dietary habits. In this section, readers will learn strategies for effectively managing these aspects of their lives.

a) Dining Out and Social Gatherings: Eating out at restaurants and attending social gatherings can present challenges for individuals on their post-surgery journey. This segment will provide practical tips for making healthier choices while dining out, such as reviewing menus in advance, opting for protein-rich options, practicing portion control, and requesting modifications when needed. Additionally, readers will gain insights into effective communication strategies to navigate social situations with confidence and assertiveness, including explaining their dietary needs and preferences to friends and family.

b) Building Supportive Relationships: The support and understanding of loved ones are crucial for long-term success. This section will explore strategies for building supportive relationships that foster a healthy and positive environment. Readers will learn how to communicate their needs effectively, educate their support network about the surgery and its dietary requirements, and enlist the support of family and friends in their journey. The chapter will also address potential challenges and provide guidance on managing unsupportive or negative influences, emphasizing the importance of setting boundaries, seeking alternative support networks, and focusing on personal growth and self-care.

6.3 Self-Care and Continued Education

Self-care and continued education play vital roles in maintaining a healthy and fulfilling lifestyle. In addition to adopting a nutritious diet, it is important to prioritize self-care practices that nurture our physical, mental, and emotional well-being. Self-care involves engaging in activities that promote relaxation, stress reduction, and overall self-improvement. This can include activities such as regular exercise, getting enough sleep, practicing mindfulness or meditation, and finding hobbies or activities that bring joy and fulfillment. Taking time for ourselves allows us to recharge and rejuvenate, enhancing our overall health and happiness.

Continued education is equally important for maintaining a healthy lifestyle. This involves staying informed and up to date with the latest research, trends, and information related to nutrition, exercise, and overall wellness. By continuously learning, we can make informed decisions about our health and make adjustments to our lifestyle as needed.

Continued education can take many forms, such as reading books, attending seminars or workshops, listening to podcasts, or following reputable sources of information online. It enables us to expand our knowledge, challenge outdated beliefs or misconceptions, and make informed choices that align with our personal health goals.

By integrating self-care and continued education into our lives, we create a solid foundation for long-term health and happiness. It is an ongoing process that requires commitment and dedication, but the rewards are well worth it. Embracing self-care and seeking knowledge empowers us to take control of our health, make positive changes, and live our lives to the fullest. Remember, self-care is not selfish; it is a necessary investment in our own well-being.

Let's look at some important points.

a) Prioritizing Self-Care: Self-care is essential for nurturing overall well-being and sustaining long-term success. This segment will discuss various self-care practices that readers can incorporate into their daily lives, such as engaging in hobbies, practicing relaxation techniques, fostering positive relationships, setting boundaries, and practicing self-compassion. The chapter will emphasize the importance of self-reflection, self-awareness, and honoring one's needs and limitations throughout the post-surgery journey.

b) Continued Education and Lifelong Learning: The journey of maintaining long-term success after gastric sleeve surgery involves continuous learning and staying informed about relevant topics. This section will encourage readers to seek ongoing education about nutrition, physical activity, behavioral strategies, and emerging research in the field. It will provide resources for accessing reliable information, such as reputable websites, books, support groups, and healthcare professionals. By staying informed, readers can make informed decisions, adapt to new evidence-based practices, and maintain a proactive approach towards their health and well-being.

c) Setting Meaningful Goals: Readers will learn about the significance of setting realistic, measurable, and non-scale goals that align with their values and aspirations. This segment will provide guidance on goal setting, tracking progress, and celebrating achievements, emphasizing the importance of recognizing and celebrating non-scale victories, such as increased energy levels, improved mobility, enhanced self-confidence, and better overall health.

d) Creating a Supportive Environment: Building a supportive environment plays a vital role in maintaining long-term success. This section will explore strategies for creating a positive and empowering support system that recognizes and celebrates individual achievements. Readers will learn how to cultivate a network of support, engage in self-reflection and self-praise, and surround themselves with positive influences that reinforce their journey and inspire continued growth.

7. EMBRACING YOUR NEW LIFE WITH GASTRIC SLEEVE SURGERY

In this final chapter, we reflect on the transformative journey gastric sleeve surgery patients have embarked upon and offer guidance on embracing their new life with confidence and positivity. It serves as a culmination of the knowledge and practical strategies shared throughout the book, empowering readers to maintain long-term success and well-being.

7.1 Celebrating Your Achievements

This section focuses on recognizing and celebrating the achievements of gastric sleeve surgery patients. It highlights the significant milestones they have reached, both physically and emotionally, since their surgery. Readers will be encouraged to reflect on their personal accomplishments, such as weight loss, improved health markers, increased energy levels, and enhanced self-confidence. The chapter emphasizes the importance of acknowledging and valuing these achievements to reinforce a positive mindset and self-esteem.

7.2 Nurturing a Positive Body Image

Maintaining a positive body image is crucial for the overall well-being and long-term success of gastric sleeve surgery patients. In this section, readers will learn practical strategies for cultivating a healthy relationship with their bodies. They will explore the concept of self-acceptance, focusing on the progress made rather than solely on physical appearance. The chapter will provide insights on setting realistic expectations, embracing body diversity, and engaging in self-care practices that promote self-love and body positivity.

7.3 Cultivating a Supportive Environment

A strong support system plays a vital role in the post-surgery journey. This section emphasizes the importance of cultivating a supportive environment that nurtures the physical, emotional, and psychological well-being of gastric sleeve surgery patients. Readers will discover strategies for communicating their needs and boundaries to loved ones, finding community support groups, and seeking professional guidance when necessary. The chapter will provide tips for navigating relationships and building a network of individuals who understand and encourage their journey.

7.4 Setting and Pursuing New Goals

Gastric sleeve surgery marks the beginning of a new chapter in life, and setting new goals is essential for continued growth and fulfillment. This section explores the process of goal setting and offers guidance on defining realistic and meaningful objectives. Readers will be encouraged to establish goals beyond weight loss, such as fitness achievements, career aspirations, travel plans, or personal development. The chapter will provide strategies for staying motivated, breaking goals into manageable steps, and celebrating progress along the way.

7.5 Sustaining a Healthy Lifestyle

Maintaining a healthy lifestyle is a lifelong commitment for gastric sleeve surgery patients. In this section, readers will receive practical advice on sustaining the positive changes they have implemented. They will explore strategies for mindful eating, regular physical activity, stress management, and self-care practices. The chapter will emphasize the importance of finding enjoyment in healthy habits and making sustainable choices that align with individual preferences and goals.

7.6 Embracing the Journey

In the final section of the book, readers will be encouraged to embrace their transformative journey with gratitude and resilience. They will reflect on the lessons learned, the strength gained, and the newfound perspective on health and well-being. The chapter will emphasize the importance of self-compassion, self-reflection, and ongoing self-improvement. Readers will be empowered to embrace their unique stories and continue their growth as they navigate their new life with gastric sleeve surgery.

As readers reach the conclusion of this book, they will possess the knowledge, tools, and inspiration to embrace their new life with gastric sleeve surgery. By celebrating achievements, nurturing a positive body image, cultivating a supportive environment, setting new goals, sustaining a healthy lifestyle, and embracing the journey, readers will embark on a fulfilling and empowered path towards long-term success and well-being.

CONCLUSION

GASTRIC SLEEVE BARIATRIC COOKBOOK is more than a book; it's your comprehensive companion for navigating the world of bariatric surgery. From surgery details to emotional support, this resource offers real-life stories and practical advice.

This guide transforms into an epic cookbook, ensuring post-surgery life is anything but dull. It covers everything from surgery to recovery, providing steadfast support like a trusted friend.

In addition, dishes suitable for post-bariatric surgery should exhibit ten essential characteristics, according to Dr. Mary L. Brandt. These include nutrient density, prioritizing protein sources, soft textures, portion control, balanced macronutrients, low sugar and fat content, fiber-rich options, hydration support, flavorful additions without excess, and customizable options.

Tailoring dishes to meet these characteristics ensures they align with the unique nutritional needs and recovery process of post-bariatric surgery individuals. Consultation with healthcare professionals or dietitians for personalized recommendations is advised. Your journey to a healthy and delicious lifestyle begins!

REAL STORIES

Sarah

My incredible journey began when I found myself at a crossroads in life. I was a woman named Sarah, and for years, I had been burdened by the weight that held me back from truly embracing life. I was unhappy, lacking confidence, and struggling to find joy in the simplest of moments. But deep within me, there was a flicker of hope, a desire for change that refused to be extinguished.

After countless failed attempts at diets and exercise programs, I stumbled upon a glimmer of hope: bariatric surgery. The idea of undergoing such a transformational procedure both terrified and excited me. It was a leap of faith, but I knew deep down that I deserved a chance at a healthier, happier life. With a mix of nervous anticipation and a newfound determination, I took the leap and underwent bariatric surgery. The day of the procedure, I remember feeling a whirlwind of emotions—fear, excitement, and an overwhelming sense of hope. Little did I know that this decision would alter the course of my life in the most incredible way.

As I woke up from surgery, a sense of relief washed over me. The journey ahead wouldn't be easy, but I was ready to embrace it wholeheartedly. With the support of my healthcare team, I learned to make healthier choices, redefine my relationship with food, and incorporate exercise into my daily routine. It wasn't about restriction; it was about nourishing my body and treating it with the love and care it deserved.

Over time, the pounds started melting away, and with each milestone, I felt a renewed sense of joy and accomplishment. The physical changes were apparent, but the most remarkable transformation happened within me. I rediscovered my confidence, my zest for life, and a newfound appreciation for the simple pleasures that had eluded me for so long. Gone were the days of hiding in oversized clothes and avoiding social situations. I embraced the world with open arms, savoring every moment of my newfound freedom. I found myself engaging in activities I had once only dreamed of—taking long walks in nature, dancing with abandon, and relishing in the sheer joy of living life to the fullest.

Today, as I reflect on my journey, I am filled with gratitude for the gift of bariatric surgery. It has not only reshaped my body but also transformed my spirit. I am no longer defined by a number on the scale, but by the happiness and fulfillment that radiates from within. To anyone who feels trapped in the clutches of excess weight, I want you to know that there is hope. Bariatric surgery is not a magic solution, but rather a tool that, when combined with determination, support, and a positive mindset, can unlock a world of possibilities. Don't let fear hold you back from embracing the life you deserve.

So, my dear friend, take that first step. Believe in yourself, trust in the process, and know that a brighter, healthier future awaits. Together, we can rewrite our stories and create a life filled with joy, self-love, and endless possibilities.

Pier

As I sat in my favorite armchair, gazing out the window, I couldn't help but feel a sense of dissatisfaction wash over me. I was a 55-year-old man named John, and for far too long, I had carried the weight of unhappiness with me—both physically and emotionally. It seemed like my high weight had taken control of my life, limiting my activities and overshadowing my confidence.

One day, as I flipped through the channels on my television, a program caught my attention. It was all about bariatric surgery—the incredible journey of individuals reclaiming their lives and finding happiness through weight loss. The stories resonated with me on a deep level, and a flicker of hope ignited within my heart.

After careful consideration and countless discussions with healthcare professionals, I made the life-altering decision to undergo bariatric surgery. It wasn't an easy choice, but I knew that it was time to take control of my health and embrace the possibilities that lay ahead. The day of the surgery was filled with a mix of nervousness and anticipation. I remember lying on the hospital bed, surrounded by a team of dedicated professionals who reassured me every step of the way. Their expertise and care gave me the confidence I needed to proceed with the procedure. As I emerged from the surgery, a wave of relief washed over me. The physical discomfort was temporary, but the newfound hope that filled my heart was immeasurable. Little did I know that this surgery would not only change my appearance but also ignite a profound transformation within me.

In the weeks and months that followed, I learned to listen to my body in a way I had never done before. The surgery served as a catalyst for positive change, motivating me to make healthier choices and embark on a journey of self-discovery. I found solace in nourishing my body with wholesome foods, embracing an active lifestyle, and seeking support from a community of individuals who understood the challenges I faced. As the pounds melted away, I discovered a renewed sense of energy and zest for life. Simple tasks that were once a struggle became easier, and I reveled in the newfound freedom that came with a healthier body. I found myself engaging in activities I had long abandoned—exploring nature trails, joining social groups, and embracing adventures that once seemed out of reach.

Today, as I reflect on my journey, I am filled with an overwhelming sense of satisfaction and happiness. Bariatric surgery was the turning point in my life—the key that unlocked a door to a world of endless possibilities. I no longer shy away from the mirror; instead, I embrace the reflection that stares back at me—a reflection of resilience, strength, and self-love.

To anyone who may be in a similar position, I want you to know that there is hope beyond the weight that burdens you. Bariatric surgery is not a magical fix, but rather a tool that, when coupled with determination and a supportive network, can empower you to reclaim your life and find true happiness.

So, my friend, if you find yourself longing for a change, take that leap of faith. Embrace the possibilities that lie within your reach. Believe in your own strength and resilience. The path may not always be easy, but the rewards are immeasurable.

I am living proof that it's never too late to rewrite your story and find fulfillment in every chapter. Today, as I step out into the world with a lighter body and a joy-filled heart, I am grateful for the transformative power of bariatric surgery. It has given me a second chance at life—one that is filled with satisfaction, happiness, and the freedom to be the best version of myself.

Linda

Allow me to share with you a remarkable and heartfelt journey that unfolded in the life of a 25-year-old woman named Linda. Like many others her age, Linda had dreams and aspirations, but her high weight and poor health seemed to cast a shadow over her potential. Her confidence dwindled, and she longed for a transformation that would set her free. Growing up, Linda struggled with her weight, battling constant self-doubt and a nagging feeling that she was missing out on the joys of life. She had tried countless diets and exercise regimens, but the results were always short-lived. It was a never-ending cycle of hope and disappointment.

One fateful day, as Linda scrolled through social media, she stumbled upon a personal story of someone who had undergone bariatric surgery. The journey they described resonated deeply within her. She saw their newfound confidence, improved health, and the genuine happiness that radiated from their smile. It was in that moment that Linda realized she had found her solution—a chance to reclaim her life. With renewed determination, Linda embarked on a thorough exploration of bariatric surgery. She sought out reputable doctors, read testimonials, and educated herself on the different procedures available. Each step brought her closer to her goal of a healthier, happier existence.

Finally, after months of research and preparation, the day of Linda's surgery arrived. Nervous excitement filled her heart as she lay on the operating table, knowing that this was the turning point she had been longing for. The skilled surgical team reassured her, and as she drifted off to sleep, a wave of hope washed over her.

Waking up in the recovery room, Linda felt a mix of emotions. She was sore and groggy, but a sense of relief and gratitude enveloped her. She knew that her life had taken a significant turn. From that moment forward, she was committed to embracing the journey of transformation. In the weeks and months that followed, Linda's dedication to her new lifestyle was unwavering. She learned to nourish her body with wholesome foods, savoring the flavors and finding joy in nutritious meals. Regular exercise became a cherished part of her routine, not as a punishment, but as a celebration of her newfound strength and vitality.

As the pounds melted away and her health dramatically improved, Linda began to witness the incredible impact of her decision. Simple tasks that were once a struggle became effortless. She reveled in the newfound energy that allowed her to fully engage in activities she had previously shied away from. Her confidence soared, and she radiated a magnetic glow that drew others towards her.

Now, as Linda reflects on her journey, she realizes that the true transformation she experienced went far beyond the physical. It was an inner metamorphosis—a blossoming of self-love, resilience, and a profound appreciation for the gift of life. She embraces each day with gratitude, knowing that she has been given a second chance to live life to the fullest. Today, Linda is a beacon of inspiration to others who are on a similar path. She offers support, encouragement, and guidance, knowing firsthand the challenges and triumphs that lie ahead. With a heart full of gratitude, she continues to embark on new adventures, create lasting memories, and inspire others to believe in the power of their own transformations.

Linda's story is a testament to the remarkable possibilities that lie within each of us. It is a reminder that no matter how bleak our circumstances may seem, there is always hope for a brighter tomorrow. With determination, support, and a steadfast belief in ourselves, we can overcome any obstacle and rewrite the narrative of our lives.

Recipes

Breakfast

Quinoa Breakfast Bowl

Servings: 1 Prep time: 10 min Cook time: 10 min

INGREDIENTS

- 3/4 cup liquid egg whites
- 1/4 cup diced bell peppers (any color)
- 1/4 cup diced tomatoes
- 1/4 cup chopped spinach
- 1/4 cup diced mushrooms
- 2 tablespoons diced onion
- Salt and pepper to taste
- Cooking spray

DIRECTIONS

1. Heat a non-stick skillet over medium heat and coat it with cooking spray.
2. Add the diced onions and bell peppers to the skillet. Sauté for 2-3 minutes until slightly softened.
3. Add the tomatoes, spinach, and mushrooms to the skillet. Cook for another 2-3 minutes until the vegetables are tender.
4. Pour the liquid egg whites into the skillet, covering the sautéed vegetables.
5. Season with salt and pepper to taste.
6. Cook for 3-4 minutes or until the egg whites are set.
7. Gently fold the omelet in half and transfer it to a plate.
8. Serve hot.

Calories: 120 - Carbohydrates: 8g - Protein: 22g - Fat: 1g

Cottage Cheese Pancakes

Servings: 1 Prep time: 10 min Cook time: 10 min

INGREDIENTS

- 1/4 cup cooked quinoa
- 1/2 cup unsweetened almond milk (or any milk of choice)
- 1/4 teaspoon vanilla extract
- 1/4 teaspoon ground cinnamon
- 1/4 cup diced fresh fruits (e.g., bananas, berries)
- 1 tablespoon chopped nuts (e.g., pecans, almonds)
- 1 teaspoon honey (optional)

DIRECTIONS

1. In a small saucepan, combine the cooked quinoa, almond milk, vanilla extract, and ground cinnamon.
2. Heat the mixture over medium heat, stirring occasionally, until it reaches a simmer.
3. Reduce the heat to low and continue cooking for about 10 minutes, or until the quinoa absorbs the liquid and becomes creamy.
4. Transfer the quinoa mixture to a bowl.
5. Top with diced fresh fruits and chopped nuts.
6. Drizzle with honey if desired.
7. Serve warm.

Calories: 180 - Carbohydrates: 24g - Protein: 6g - Fat: 6g

Green Protein Smoothie

Servings: 1　　　Prep time: 10 min　　　Cook time: /

INGREDIENTS

- 1 cup unsweetened almond milk (or any milk of choice)
- 1/2 ripe banana
- 1/2 cup fresh spinach leaves
- 1/4 cup diced cucumber
- 1/4 cup diced pineapple
- 1 tablespoon chia seeds
- Ice cubes (optional)

DIRECTIONS

1. In a blender, combine the almond milk, banana, spinach, cucumber, pineapple, and chia seeds.
2. Blend until smooth and creamy.
3. Add ice cubes if desired and blend again until well combined.
4. Pour into a glass and serve chilled.

Calories: 150 - Carbohydrates: 26g - Protein: 6g - Fat: 4g

Avocado Toast

Servings: 1　　　Prep time: 10 min　　　Cook time: 10 min

INGREDIENTS

- 1 slice whole-grain bread, toasted
- 1/4 ripe avocado
- 1/2 teaspoon lemon juice
- Pinch of salt
- Pinch of black pepper
- Optional toppings: sliced tomatoes, fresh herbs, or a sprinkle of red pepper flakes

DIRECTIONS

1. Mash the ripe avocado in a small bowl.
2. Add lemon juice, salt, and black pepper. Mix well.
3. Spread the avocado mixture evenly onto the toasted bread.
4. Add any desired toppings, such as sliced tomatoes, fresh herbs, or a sprinkle of red pepper flakes.
5. Serve immediately.

Calories: 120 - Carbohydrates: 13g - Protein: 3g - Fat: 7g

Protein-Packed Breakfast Burrito

Servings: 1   Prep time: 10 min   Cook time: 10 min

INGREDIENTS

- 1 whole wheat tortilla (6-8 inches in diameter)
- 2 large eggs
- 1/4 cup black beans, rinsed and drained
- 1/4 cup diced bell peppers (any color)
- 2 tablespoons diced onion
- 2 tablespoons shredded low-fat cheese
- Salt and pepper to taste
- Cooking spray

DIRECTIONS

1. In a small bowl whisk the eggs and season with salt and pepper.
2. Heat a non-stick skillet over medium heat and coat it with cooking spray.
3. Add the diced onions and bell peppers to the skillet. Sauté for 2-3 minutes until slightly softened.
4. Pour the whisked eggs into the skillet and scramble them with the sautéed vegetables.
5. Once the eggs are cooked, remove the skillet from heat.
6. Warm the tortilla in a separate skillet or in the microwave for a few seconds.
7. Place the scrambled eggs in the center of the tortilla.
8. Top with black beans and shredded cheese.
9. Fold the sides of the tortilla over the filling and roll it up into a burrito.
10. Serve hot.

Calories: 310 - Carbohydrates: 30g - Protein: 23g - Fat: 10g

Chia Seed Pudding

Servings: 2   Prep time: 5 min   Cook time: /

INGREDIENTS

- 1/4 cup chia seeds
- 1 cup unsweetened almond milk (or any milk of choice)
- 1 tablespoon honey or maple syrup
- 1/2 teaspoon vanilla extract
- Optional toppings: fresh fruits, chopped nuts, or a sprinkle of cinnamon

DIRECTIONS

1. In a bowl, combine the chia seeds, almond milk, honey or maple syrup, and vanilla extract. Mix well.
2. Cover the bowl and refrigerate overnight or for at least 4-6 hours, allowing the chia seeds to absorb the liquid and thicken.
3. Stir the chia pudding before serving to ensure a smooth consistency.
4. Divide the pudding into serving bowls or glasses.
5. Top with your choice of fresh fruits, chopped nuts, or a sprinkle of cinnamon.
6. Serve chilled.

Calories: 180 - Carbohydrates: 18g - Protein: 5g - Fat: 9g

Protein Pancakes

Servings: 2   Prep time: 10 min   Cook time: 10 min

INGREDIENTS

- 1/2 cup oat flour
- 1 scoop vanilla protein powder
- 1 teaspoon baking powder
- 1/2 teaspoon cinnamon
- 1/2 cup unsweetened almond milk (or any milk of choice)
- 1 large egg
- 1/2 teaspoon vanilla extract
- Cooking spray

DIRECTIONS

1. In a mixing bowl, combine the oat flour, protein powder, baking powder, and cinnamon. Mix well.
2. In a separate bowl, whisk together the almond milk, egg, and vanilla extract.
3. Pour the wet ingredients into the dry ingredients and stir until well combined.
4. Heat a non-stick skillet or griddle over medium heat and coat it with cooking spray.
5. Pour 1/4 cup of the pancake batter onto the skillet for each pancake.
6. Cook for 2-3 minutes, or until bubbles form on the surface.
7. Flip the pancakes and cook for another 1-2 minutes, or until golden brown.
8. Repeat with the remaining batter.
9. Serve warm with a drizzle of sugar-free syrup or a dollop of Greek yogurt.

Calories: 230 - Carbohydrates: 21g - Protein: 25g - Fat: 5g

Berry Protein Smoothie Bowl

Servings: 1   Prep time: 5 min   Cook time: /

INGREDIENTS

- 1/2 cup frozen mixed berries
- 1/2 ripe banana
- 1/2 cup unsweetened almond milk (or any milk of choice)
- 1 scoop vanilla protein powder
- Toppings: sliced fresh fruits, granola, shredded coconut, or a sprinkle of chia seeds

DIRECTIONS

1. In a blender, combine the frozen berries, banana, almond milk, and vanilla protein powder.
2. Blend until smooth and creamy.
3. Pour the smoothie into a bowl.
4. Top with your choice of sliced fresh fruits, granola, shredded coconut, or a sprinkle of chia seeds.
5. Serve immediately.

Calories: 250 - Carbohydrates: 30g - Protein: 25g - Fat: 5g

Lunch

Grilled Chicken Salad

Servings: 2   Prep time: 15 min   Cook time: 15 min

INGREDIENTS

- 8 ounces boneless, skinless chicken breast
- 4 cups mixed salad greens
- 1/2 cup cherry tomatoes, halved
- 1/4 cup cucumber, sliced
- 1/4 cup red onion, thinly sliced
- 2 tablespoons balsamic vinaigrette
- Salt and pepper to taste

DIRECTIONS

1. Preheat the grill to medium heat.
2. Season the chicken breast with salt and pepper.
3. Grill the chicken for 6-8 minutes per side, or until cooked through.
4. Let the chicken rest for a few minutes, then slice it into thin strips.
5. In a large bowl, combine the salad greens, cherry tomatoes, cucumber, and red onion.
6. Drizzle the balsamic vinaigrette over the salad and toss to coat.
7. Divide the salad onto plates and top with the grilled chicken.
8. Serve immediately.

Calories: 220 - Carbohydrates: 9g - Protein: 30g - Fat: 6g

Berry Protein Smoothie Bowl

Servings: 1   Prep time: 5 min   Cook time: /

INGREDIENTS

- 1/2 cup frozen mixed berries
- 1/2 ripe banana
- 1/2 cup unsweetened almond milk (or any milk of choice)
- 1 scoop vanilla protein powder
- Toppings: sliced fresh fruits, granola, shredded coconut, or a sprinkle of chia seeds

DIRECTIONS

1. In a blender, combine the frozen berries, banana, almond milk, and vanilla protein powder.
2. Blend until smooth and creamy.
3. Pour the smoothie into a bowl.
4. Top with your choice of sliced fresh fruits, granola, shredded coconut, or a sprinkle of chia seeds.
5. Serve immediately.

Calories: 250 - Carbohydrates: 30g - Protein: 25g - Fat: 5g

Turkey Lettuce Wraps

Servings: 4   Prep time: 15 min   Cook time: 10 min

INGREDIENTS

- 1 pound lean ground turkey
- 2 cloves garlic, minced
- 1 teaspoon ground ginger
- 2 tablespoons reduced-sodium soy sauce
- 1 tablespoon hoisin sauce
- 1 tablespoon sesame oil
- 1/4 cup green onions, chopped
- 8 large lettuce leaves (such as iceberg or butter lettuce)

DIRECTIONS

1. In a large skillet, cook the ground turkey over medium heat until browned and cooked through.
2. Add the minced garlic and ground ginger to the skillet. Cook for an additional 1-2 minutes.
3. Stir in the soy sauce, hoisin sauce, sesame oil, and chopped green onions. Cook for another 2 minutes.
4. Remove the skillet from heat.
5. Spoon the turkey mixture onto the lettuce leaves.
6. Roll up the leaves like a burrito, tucking in the sides as you go.
7. Serve immediately.

Calories: 180 - Carbohydrates: 5g - Protein: 24g - Fat: 7g

Salmon and Quinoa Salad

Servings: 2   Prep time: 15 min   Cook time: 20 min

INGREDIENTS

- 8 ounces salmon fillet
- 1 cup cooked quinoa
- 2 cups mixed salad greens
- 1/2 cup cherry tomatoes, halved
- 1/4 cup red bell pepper, diced
- 2 tablespoons lemon juice
- 1 tablespoon olive oil
- Salt and pepper to taste

DIRECTIONS

1. Preheat the oven to 400°F (200°C).
2. Place the salmon fillet on a baking sheet lined with parchment paper. Season with salt and pepper.
3. Bake the salmon for 12-15 minutes, or until cooked through.
4. Remove the salmon from the oven and let it cool slightly. Flake the salmon into small pieces
5. In a large bowl, combine the cooked quinoa, mixed salad greens, cherry tomatoes, and red bell pepper.
6. In a small bowl, whisk together the lemon juice, olive oil, salt, and pepper to make the dressing.
7. Pour the dressing over the quinoa salad and toss to coat.
8. Divide the salad onto plates and top with the flaked salmon.
9. Serve immediately.

Calories: 320 - Carbohydrates: 25g - Protein: 28g - Fat: 12g

Caprese Stuffed Chicken Breast

Servings: 2　　　　Prep time: 15 min　　　　Cook time: 25 min

INGREDIENTS

- 2 boneless, skinless chicken breasts
- 2 slices fresh mozzarella cheese
- 4 large basil leaves
- 2 slices tomato
- 1 tablespoon olive oil
- Salt and pepper to taste

DIRECTIONS

1. Preheat the oven to 375°F (190°C).
2. Butterfly the chicken breasts by cutting horizontally through the center, leaving one side intact.
3. Open the chicken breasts like a book.
4. Season the inside of the chicken breasts with salt and pepper.
5. Place a slice of mozzarella cheese, two basil leaves, and a slice of tomato on one side of each chicken breast.
6. Fold the other side of the chicken breast over the filling, pressing the edges together to seal.
7. Heat olive oil in an oven-safe skillet over medium heat.
8. Add the stuffed chicken breasts to the skillet and cook for 2-3 minutes on each side until browned.
9. Transfer the skillet to the preheated oven and bake for 15-18 minutes or until the chicken is cooked through.
10. Remove from the oven and let the chicken rest for a few minutes before serving.

Calories: 280 - Carbohydrates: 4g - Protein: 38g - Fat: 12g

Shrimp and Avocado Salad

Servings: 2　　　　Prep time: 15 min　　　　Cook time: 20 min

INGREDIENTS

- 8 ounces shrimp, peeled and deveined
- 1/2 avocado, diced
- 2 cups mixed salad greens
- 1/4 cup red onion, thinly sliced
- 1/4 cup cherry tomatoes, halved
- 2 tablespoons lime juice
- 1 tablespoon olive oil
- Salt and pepper to taste

DIRECTIONS

1. Heat olive oil in a skillet over medium heat.
2. Add the shrimp to the skillet and cook for 2-3 minutes on each side until pink and cooked through.
3. Remove the shrimp from heat and let them cool slightly.
4. In a large bowl, combine the mixed salad greens, red onion, and cherry tomatoes.
5. Add the diced avocado and cooked shrimp to the bowl.
6. In a small bowl, whisk together the lime juice, olive oil, salt, and pepper to make the dressing.
7. Drizzle the dressing over the salad and toss to coat.
8. Divide the salad onto plates and serve immediately.

Calories: 220 - Carbohydrates: 8g - Protein: 24g - Fat: 10g

Turkey and Vegetable Stir-Fry

Servings: 2 Prep time: 10 min Cook time: 15 min

INGREDIENTS

- 8 ounces lean ground turkey
- 1 cup broccoli florets
- 1/2 cup snap peas
- 1/2 cup sliced bell peppers
- 1/4 cup shredded carrots
- 2 cloves garlic, minced
- 1 tablespoon low-sodium soy sauce
- 1 tablespoon sesame oil
- Salt and pepper to taste

DIRECTIONS

1. Heat sesame oil in a large skillet or wok over medium heat.
2. Add minced garlic and sauté for 1 minute.
3. Add ground turkey to the skillet and cook until browned and cooked through.
4. Add broccoli florets, snap peas, bell peppers, and shredded carrots to the skillet. Stir-fry for 5-6 minutes until vegetables are tender-crisp.
5. Stir in low-sodium soy sauce and season with salt and pepper to taste.
6. Cook for an additional 2-3 minutes, then remove from heat.
7. Divide the stir-fry onto plates and serve immediately.

Calories: 220- Carbohyd rates: 12g - Protein: 26g - Fat: 9g

Greek Chicken Salad

Servings: 2 Prep time: 15 min Cook time: 15 min

INGREDIENTS

- 8 ounces boneless, skinless chicken breast
- 4 cups mixed salad greens
- 1/2 cup cherry tomatoes, halved
- 1/4 cup cucumber, diced
- 1/4 cup red onion, thinly sliced
- 2 tablespoons feta cheese, crumbled
- 1 tablespoon lemon juice
- 1 tablespoon extra-virgin olive oil
- 1/2 teaspoon dried oregano
- Salt and pepper to taste

DIRECTIONS

1. Preheat the oven to 400°F (200°C).
2. Season the chicken breast with dried oregano, salt, and pepper.
3. Place the chicken breast on a baking sheet lined with parchment paper and bake for 18-20 minutes or until cooked through.
4. Remove the chicken from the oven and let it cool slightly. Slice the chicken into thin strips.
5. In a large bowl, combine the mixed salad greens, cherry tomatoes, cucumber, and red onion.
6. In a small bowl, whisk together the lemon juice, extra-virgin olive oil, salt, and pepper to make the dressing.
7. Pour the dressing over the salad and toss to coat.
8. Divide the salad onto plates and top with the sliced chicken and crumbled feta cheese.
9. Serve immediately.

Calories: 240 - Carbohydrates: 9g - Protein: 30g - Fat: 10g

Spinach and Feta Stuffed Chicken Breast

Servings: 2　　　Prep time: 25 min　　　Cook time: 15 min

INGREDIENTS

- 2 boneless, skinless chicken breasts
- 2 cups fresh spinach leaves
- 1/4 cup crumbled feta cheese
- 2 tablespoons sun-dried tomatoes, chopped

DIRECTIONS

1. Preheat the oven to 375°F (190°C).
2. Butterfly the chicken breasts by cutting horizontally through the center, leaving one side intact.
3. Open the chicken breasts like a book.
4. Season the inside of the chicken breasts with salt and pepper.
5. Layer spinach leaves, crumbled feta cheese, and sun-dried tomatoes on one side of each chicken breast.
6. Fold the other side of the chicken breast over the filling, pressing the edges together to seal.
7. Heat olive oil in an oven-safe skillet over medium heat.
8. Add the stuffed chicken breasts to the skillet and cook for 2-3 minutes on each side until browned.
9. Transfer the skillet to the preheated oven and bake for 20-25 minutes or until the chicken is cooked through.
10. Remove from the oven and let the chicken rest for a few minutes before serving.

Calories: 290 - Carbohydrates: 2g - Protein: 38g - Fat: 14g

Tuna Salad Lettuce Wraps

Servings: 2　　　Prep time: 15 min　　　Cook time: /

INGREDIENTS

- 1 can (5 ounces) tuna in water, drained
- 1/4 cup celery, diced
- 1/4 cup red onion, diced
- 2 tablespoons mayonnaise (low-fat or light)
- 1 tablespoon lemon juice
- Salt and pepper to taste
- 4 large lettuce leaves

DIRECTIONS

1. In a bowl, combine tuna, celery, red onion, mayonnaise, lemon juice, salt, and pepper. Mix well.
2. Place a scoop of the tuna salad mixture onto each lettuce leaf.
3. Roll up the lettuce leaf, enclosing the filling.
4. Serve immediately.

Calories: 140 - Carbohydrates: 5g - Protein: 18g - Fat: 5g

Zucchini Noodles with Grilled Chicken

Servings: 2   Prep time: 15 min   Cook time: 10 min

INGREDIENTS

- 2 medium zucchini
- 8 ounces boneless, skinless chicken breast
- 2 tablespoons olive oil, divided
- 2 cloves garlic, minced
- 1/4 teaspoon red pepper flakes (optional)
- Salt and pepper to taste
- Fresh basil leaves, for garnish

DIRECTIONS

1. Using a spiralizer or vegetable peeler, create zucchini noodles from the zucchini. Set aside.
2. Preheat a grill or grill pan over medium-high heat.
3. Season the chicken breast with salt, pepper, and red pepper flakes (if using).
4. Drizzle 1 tablespoon of olive oil over the chicken breast and massage it in to coat.
5. Grill the chicken for 4-5 minutes on each side or until cooked through.
6. Remove the chicken from the grill and let it rest for a few minutes. Slice the chicken into thin strips.
7. In a large skillet, heat the remaining tablespoon of olive oil over medium heat.
8. Add minced garlic to the skillet and sauté for 1 minute until fragrant.
9. Add the zucchini noodles to the skillet and cook for 2-3 minutes until they are tender but still crisp.
10. Season the zucchini noodles with salt and pepper to taste.
11. Divide the zucchini noodles onto plates and top with the grilled chicken strips.
12. Garnish with fresh basil leaves and serve immediately

Calories: 280 - Carbohydrates: 10g - Protein: 30g - Fat: 14g

Caprese Salad Skewers

Servings: 2   Prep time: 15 min   Cook time: /

INGREDIENTS

- 12 cherry tomatoes
- 12 small fresh mozzarella balls
- 12 fresh basil leaves
- 1 tablespoon balsamic glaze
- 1 tablespoon extra-virgin olive oil
- Salt and pepper to taste

DIRECTIONS

1. Thread a cherry tomato, a mozzarella ball, and a basil leaf onto a skewer.
2. Repeat with the remaining ingredients to make a total of 6 skewers.
3. Drizzle the skewers with balsamic glaze and olive oil.
4. Season with salt and pepper to taste.
5. Serve immediately.

Calories: 180- Carbohydrates: 4g - Protein: 12g - Fat: 13g

Mexican Chicken Soup

Servings: 4 Prep time: 15 min Cook time: 25 min

INGREDIENTS

- 8 ounces boneless, skinless chicken breast, cooked and shredded
- 1 tablespoon olive oil
- 1/2 cup diced onion
- 2 cloves garlic, minced
- 1 jalapeño, seeded and minced
- 1 can (14 ounces) diced tomatoes, with juice
- 4 cups low-sodium chicken broth
- 1 teaspoon ground cumin
- 1 teaspoon chili powder
- Salt and pepper to taste
- Fresh cilantro, chopped, for garnish
- Lime wedges, for serving

DIRECTIONS

1. Heat olive oil in a large pot over medium heat.
2. Add diced onion, minced garlic, and minced jalapeño to the pot. Sauté for 2-3 minutes until the vegetables are softened.
3. Add diced tomatoes (with juice) to the pot and stir to combine.
4. Pour in the chicken broth and add ground cumin and chili powder. Stir well.
5. Bring the soup to a boil, then reduce heat and simmer for 15 minutes.
6. Add the shredded chicken to the pot and simmer for an additional 5 minutes to heat through.
7. Season the soup with salt and pepper to taste.
8. Ladle the soup into bowls, garnish with fresh cilantro, and serve with lime wedges on the side.

Calories: 180 - Carbohydrates: 8g - Protein: 20g - Fat: 7g

Turkey Lettuce Wrap

Servings: 2 Prep time: 15 min Cook time: /

INGREDIENTS

- 8 ounces lean ground turkey
- 1/2 cup diced bell peppers
- 1/4 cup diced red onion
- 2 tablespoons low-sodium soy sauce
- 1 tablespoon sesame oil
- 1 teaspoon minced ginger
- 4 large lettuce leaves

DIRECTIONS

1. Heat sesame oil in a skillet over medium heat.
2. Add ground turkey to the skillet and cook until browned and cooked through.
3. Add diced bell peppers, diced red onion, and minced ginger to the skillet. Sauté for 2-3 minutes until the vegetables are tender.
4. Stir in low-sodium soy sauce and cook for an additional minute.
5. Divide the turkey mixture onto the lettuce leaves and roll them up like a wrap.
6. Serve immediately.

Calories: 210 - Carbohydrates: 7g - Protein: 26g - Fat: 9g

Quinoa Salad with Grilled Shrimp

Servings: 2   Prep time: 15 min   Cook time: 10 min

INGREDIENTS

- 8 ounces shrimp, peeled and deveined
- 1/2 cup cooked quinoa
- 1/4 cup cherry tomatoes, halved
- 1/4 cup cucumber, diced
- 2 tablespoons red onion, thinly sliced
- 2 tablespoons fresh parsley, chopped
- 1 tablespoon lemon juice
- 1 tablespoon extra-virgin olive oil
- Salt and pepper to taste

DIRECTIONS

1. Preheat a grill or grill pan over medium-high heat.
2. Season the shrimp with salt and pepper.
3. Grill the shrimp for 2-3 minutes on each side until cooked through.
4. In a large bowl, combine cooked quinoa, cherry tomatoes, cucumber, red onion, and fresh parsley.
5. In a small bowl, whisk together lemon juice, extra-virgin olive oil, salt, and pepper to make the dressing.
6. Pour the dressing over the quinoa salad and toss to coat.
7. Divide the salad onto plates and top with the grilled shrimp.
8. Serve immediately.

Calories: 230 - Carbohydrates: 16g - Protein: 26g - Fat: 7g

Egg Salad Lettuce Wraps

Servings: 2   Prep time: 15 min   Cook time: /

INGREDIENTS

- 4 hard-boiled eggs, peeled and chopped
- 1/4 cup diced celery
- 1/4 cup diced red onion
- 2 tablespoons mayonnaise (low-fat or light)
- 1 tablespoon Dijon mustard
- 1 tablespoon fresh dill, chopped
- Salt and pepper to taste
- 4 large lettuce leaves

DIRECTIONS

1. In a bowl, combine chopped hard-boiled eggs, diced celery, diced red onion, mayonnaise, Dijon mustard, fresh dill, salt, and pepper. Mix well.
2. Place a scoop of the egg salad mixture onto each lettuce leaf.
3. Roll up the lettuce leaf, enclosing the filling.
4. Serve immediately.

Calories: 220 - Carbohydrates: 4g - Protein: 13g - Fat: 17g

Greek Chicken Salad

Servings: 2   Prep time: 15 min   Cook time: 10 min

INGREDIENTS

- 8 ounces boneless, skinless chicken breast
- 2 cups mixed salad greens
- 1/4 cup sliced cucumber
- 1/4 cup cherry tomatoes, halved
- 2 tablespoons sliced Kalamata olives
- 2 tablespoons crumbled feta cheese
- 1 tablespoon extra-virgin olive oil
- 1 tablespoon lemon juice
- 1 teaspoon dried oregano
- Salt and pepper to taste

DIRECTIONS

1. Season the chicken breast with salt, pepper, and dried oregano.
2. Grill or cook the chicken in a skillet over medium-high heat until cooked through. Let it cool, then slice into strips.
3. In a bowl, combine mixed salad greens, sliced cucumber, cherry tomatoes, Kalamata olives, and crumbled feta cheese.
4. In a small bowl, whisk together extra-virgin olive oil, lemon juice, salt, and pepper to make the dressing.
5. Add the sliced chicken to the salad and drizzle with the dressing. Toss to combine.
6. Divide the salad onto plates and serve.

Calories: 240 - Carbohydrates: 6g - Protein: 28g - Fat: 11g

Zucchini Noodles with Turkey Meatballs

Servings: 2   Prep time: 20 min   Cook time: 25 min

INGREDIENTS

For the Turkey Meatballs:
- 8 ounces ground turkey
- 1/4 cup grated Parmesan cheese
- 1/4 cup almond flour
- 1/4 cup finely chopped fresh parsley
- 1/4 cup finely chopped onion
- 1 clove garlic, minced
- 1 large egg, beaten
- 1/2 teaspoon dried oregano
- Salt and pepper to taste

For the Zucchini Noodles:
- 2 medium zucchini, spiralized
- 1 tablespoon olive oil
- 1 cup marinara sauce (sugar-free)
- Fresh basil leaves, for garnish

DIRECTIONS

1. Preheat the oven to 400°F (200°C) and line a baking sheet with parchment paper.
2. In a bowl, combine ground turkey, grated Parmesan cheese, almond flour, chopped fresh parsley, chopped onion, minced garlic, beaten egg, dried oregano, salt, and pepper. Mix well.
3. Roll the turkey mixture into small meatballs and place them on the prepared baking sheet.
4. Bake the meatballs in the preheated oven for 15-20 minutes until cooked through.
5. In a skillet, heat olive oil over medium heat. Add spiralized zucchini and sauté for 3-4 minutes until tender.
6. Pour marinara sauce over the zucchini noodles and stir to coat.
7. Divide the zucchini noodles onto plates and top with turkey meatballs.
8. Garnish with fresh basil leaves and serve.

Calories: 260 - Carbohydrates: 12g - Protein: 25g - Fat: 13g

Tuna Avocado Lettuce Wraps

Servings: 2   Prep time: 15 min   Cook time: /

INGREDIENTS

- 1 can (5 ounces) tuna in water, drained
- 1/2 ripe avocado mashed
- 2 tablespoons diced red onion
- 2 tablespoons diced celery
- 1 tablespoon lemon juice
- Salt and pepper to taste
- 4 large lettuce leaves

DIRECTIONS

1. In a bowl, combine drained tuna, mashed avocado, diced red onion, diced celery, lemon juice, salt, and pepper. Mix well.
2. Place a scoop of the tuna mixture onto each lettuce leaf.
3. Roll up the lettuce leaf, enclosing the filling.
4. Serve immediately.

Calories: 180 - Carbohydrates: 8g - Protein: 20g - Fat: 8g

Caprese Stuffed Portobello Mushrooms

Servings: 2   Prep time: 20 min   Cook time: 15 min

INGREDIENTS

- 2 large portobello mushroom caps
- 4 slices fresh mozzarella cheese
- 4 slices tomato
- 4 fresh basil leaves
- 1 tablespoon balsamic glaze
- Salt and pepper to taste

DIRECTIONS

1. Preheat the oven to 400°F (200°C) and line a baking sheet with parchment paper.
2. Remove the stems from the portobello mushroom caps and clean them.
3. Season the mushroom caps with salt and pepper.
4. Place the mushroom caps on the prepared baking sheet.
5. Top each mushroom cap with 2 slices of fresh mozzarella cheese, 2 slices of tomato, and 2 fresh basil leaves.
6. Drizzle balsamic glaze over the stuffed mushrooms.
7. Bake in the preheated oven for 12-15 minutes until the cheese is melted and bubbly.
8. Remove from the oven and let them cool slightly before serving.

Calories: 180 - Carbohydrates: 7g - Protein: 15g - Fat: 10g

Chicken and Vegetable Stir-Fry

Servings: 2   Prep time: 15 min   Cook time: 15 min

INGREDIENTS

- 8 ounces boneless, skinless chicken breast, sliced
- 1 cup broccoli florets
- 1/2 cup sliced bell peppers
- 1/2 cup sliced zucchini
- 1/4 cup sliced carrots
- 2 tablespoons low-sodium soy sauce
- 1 tablespoon olive oil
- 1 teaspoon minced garlic
- 1/2 teaspoon grated ginger
- Salt and pepper to taste

DIRECTIONS

1. In a skillet or wok, heat olive oil over medium-high heat.
2. Add sliced chicken breast and cook until browned and cooked through. Remove from the skillet and set aside.
3. In the same skillet, add minced garlic and grated ginger. Sauté for 1 minute until fragrant.
4. Add broccoli florets, sliced bell peppers, sliced zucchini, and sliced carrots to the skillet. Stir-fry for 5-7 minutes until the vegetables are tender-crisp.
5. Return the cooked chicken to the skillet and pour in low-sodium soy sauce. Stir to coat everything evenly.
6. Cook for an additional 2-3 minutes until the chicken and vegetables are heated through.
7. Season with salt and pepper to taste.
8. Serve immediately.

Calories: 220 - Carbohydrates: 8g - Protein: 30g - Fat: 7g

Salmon and Asparagus Foil Pack

Servings: 2   Prep time: 20 min   Cook time: 20 min

INGREDIENTS

- 2 4-ounce salmon fillets
- 10-12 asparagus spears, trimmed
- 1 tablespoon olive oil
- 1 teaspoon minced garlic
- 1/2 teaspoon dried dill
- Salt and pepper to taste
- Lemon wedges, for serving

DIRECTIONS

1. Preheat the oven to 400°F (200°C).
2. Place each salmon fillet on a separate piece of aluminum foil.
3. Arrange asparagus spears around the salmon fillets.
4. Drizzle olive oil over the salmon and asparagus.
5. Sprinkle minced garlic, dried dill, salt, and pepper over the top.
6. Fold the aluminum foil to create a sealed packet.
7. Place the foil packets on a baking sheet and bake in the preheated oven for 15-20 minutes until the salmon is cooked through and the asparagus is tender.
8. Carefully open the foil packets and serve with lemon wedges.

Calories: 280 - Carbohydrates: 5g - Protein: 28g - Fat: 17g

Turkey and Vegetable Lettuce Wraps

Servings: 2　　　Prep time: 15 min　　　Cook time: 10 min

INGREDIENTS

- 8 ounces ground turkey
- 1/2 cup diced bell peppers
- 1/4 cup diced onion
- 1/4 cup diced zucchini
- 1 clove garlic, minced
- 2 tablespoons low-sodium soy sauce
- 1 tablespoon olive oil
- 4 large lettuce leaves

DIRECTIONS

1. In a skillet, heat olive oil over medium heat.
2. Add ground turkey and cook until browned and cooked through. Break up the meat into crumbles.
3. Add diced bell peppers, diced onion, diced zucchini, and minced garlic to the skillet. Cook for 3-4 minutes until the vegetables are tender.
4. Pour low-sodium soy sauce over the turkey and vegetable mixture. Stir to combine and cook for an additional 2 minutes.
5. Remove from heat and let it cool slightly.
6. Spoon the turkey and vegetable mixture onto each lettuce leaf.
7. Roll up the lettuce leaf, enclosing the filling.
8. Serve immediately.

Calories: 200 - Carbohydrates: 8g - Protein: 24g - Fat: 8g

Quinoa and Black Bean Salad

Servings: 4　　　Prep time: 20 min　　　Cook time: 20 min

INGREDIENTS

- 1 cup cooked quinoa
- 1 can (15 ounces) black beans, rinsed and drained
- 1 cup diced tomatoes
- 1/2 cup diced red bell pepper
- 1/4 cup diced red onion
- 1/4 cup chopped fresh cilantro
- 2 tablespoons lime juice
- 2 tablespoons olive oil
- 1 teaspoon ground cumin
- Salt and pepper to taste

DIRECTIONS

1. In a large bowl, combine cooked quinoa, black beans, diced tomatoes, diced red bell pepper, diced red onion, and chopped fresh cilantro.
2. In a small bowl, whisk together lime juice, olive oil, ground cumin, salt, and pepper to make the dressing.
3. Pour the dressing over the quinoa and black bean mixture. Toss to combine.
4. Refrigerate the salad for at least 30 minutes to allow the flavors to meld.
5. Serve chilled.

Calories: 220 - Carbohydrates: 30g - Protein: 9g - Fat: 8g

Egg and Vegetable Muffins

Servings: 6 Prep time: 15 min Cook time: 20 min

INGREDIENTS

- 6 large eggs
- 1/2 cup diced bell peppers
- 1/2 cup diced zucchini
- 1/4 cup diced onion
- 1/4 cup diced mushrooms
- 1/4 cup shredded cheddar cheese
- 1 tablespoon chopped fresh parsley
- Salt and pepper to taste

DIRECTIONS

1. Preheat the oven to 350°F (175°C) and grease a muffin tin.
2. In a bowl, whisk the eggs until well beaten.
3. Add diced bell peppers, diced zucchini, diced onion, diced mushrooms, shredded cheddar cheese, chopped fresh parsley, salt, and pepper to the bowl. Mix well.
4. Pour the egg and vegetable mixture evenly into the greased muffin tin.
5. Bake in the preheated oven for 15-20 minutes until the muffins are set and golden brown on top.
6. Remove from the oven and let them cool slightly before serving.

Calories: 90 - Carbohydrates: 3g - Protein: 7g - Fat: 6g

Spinach and Feta Stuffed Chicken Breast

Servings: 2 Prep time: 20 min Cook time: 25 min

INGREDIENTS

- 2 boneless, skinless chicken breasts
- 1 cup fresh spinach leaves
- 1/4 cup crumbled feta cheese
- 1 tablespoon olive oil
- 1 teaspoon minced garlic
- 1/2 teaspoon dried oregano
- Salt and pepper to taste

DIRECTIONS

1. Preheat the oven to 400°F (200°C) and line a baking dish with parchment paper.
2. Butterfly the chicken breasts by making a lengthwise cut through the center, stopping about 1/4 inch from the other side.
3. Open the chicken breasts and lay them flat.
4. In a bowl, combine fresh spinach leaves, crumbled feta cheese, olive oil, minced garlic, dried oregano, salt, and pepper.
5. Spread the spinach and feta mixture evenly on one side of each chicken breast.
6. Fold the other side of the chicken breast over the filling, creating a stuffed chicken breast.
7. Place the stuffed chicken breasts in the prepared baking dish.
8. Bake in the preheated oven for 20-25 minutes until the chicken is cooked through and no longer pink in the center.
9. Remove from the oven and let them rest for a few minutes before serving.

Calories: 280 - Carbohydrates: 2g - Protein: 40g - Fat: 12g

Dinner

Baked Lemon Herb Chicken

Servings: 2　　　Prep time: 15 min　　　Cook time: 25 min

INGREDIENTS

- 2 boneless, skinless chicken breasts
- 1 tablespoon olive oil
- 1 tablespoon lemon juice
- 1 teaspoon dried thyme
- 1 teaspoon dried rosemary
- Salt and pepper to taste

DIRECTIONS

1. Preheat the oven to 400°F (200°C) and line a baking dish with parchment paper.
2. Place the chicken breasts in the baking dish.
3. In a small bowl, mix together olive oil, lemon juice, dried thyme, dried rosemary, salt, and pepper.
4. Drizzle the mixture over the chicken breasts, ensuring they are well coated.
5. Bake in the preheated oven for 20-25 minutes until the chicken is cooked through and no longer pink in the center.
6. Remove from the oven and let the chicken rest for a few minutes before serving.

Calories: 180 - Carbohydrates: 1g - Protein: 25g - Fat: 8g

Zucchini Noodles with Shrimp

Servings: 2　　　Prep time: 20 min　　　Cook time: 10 min

INGREDIENTS

- 2 medium zucchini
- 8 ounces peeled and deveined shrimp
- 2 tablespoons olive oil
- 2 cloves garlic, minced
- 1/4 teaspoon red pepper flakes
- Salt and pepper to taste
- 2 tablespoons grated Parmesan cheese
- Chopped fresh parsley for garnish

DIRECTIONS

1. Use a spiralizer or vegetable peeler to create zucchini noodles from the zucchini. Set aside.
2. In a large skillet, heat olive oil over medium heat.
3. Add minced garlic and red pepper flakes to the skillet. Sauté for 1 minute until fragrant.
4. Add shrimp to the skillet and cook for 3-4 minutes until pink and cooked through.
5. Season with salt and pepper to taste.
6. Add the zucchini noodles to the skillet and toss them with the shrimp and garlic mixture.
7. Cook for 2-3 minutes until the zucchini noodles are tender but still slightly crisp.
8. Remove from heat and sprinkle grated Parmesan cheese over the top.
9. Garnish with chopped fresh parsley before serving.

Calories: 210 - Carbohydrates: 6g - Protein: 25g - Fat: 10g

Turkey Meatballs with Marinara Sauce

Servings: 4   Prep time: 15 min   Cook time: 25 min

INGREDIENTS

- 1 pound ground turkey
- 1/4 cup grated Parmesan cheese
- 1/4 cup almond flour
- 1/4 cup chopped fresh parsley
- 1/4 cup chopped onion
- 1 clove garlic, minced
- 1 egg, beaten
- 1 teaspoon dried oregano
- 1 teaspoon dried basil
- Salt and pepper to taste
- 2 cups low-sugar marinara sauce

DIRECTIONS

1. Preheat the oven to 400°F (200°C) and line a baking sheet with parchment paper.
2. In a large bowl, combine ground turkey, grated Parmesan cheese, almond flour, chopped fresh parsley, chopped onion, minced garlic, beaten egg, dried oregano, dried basil, salt, and pepper. Mix well.
3. Roll the mixture into meatballs, approximately 1 inch in diameter, and place them on the prepared baking sheet.
4. Bake in the preheated oven for 20-25 minutes until the meatballs are cooked through and browned.
5. In a separate saucepan, heat the marinara sauce over medium heat until warmed.
6. Serve the turkey meatballs with the marinara sauce.

Calories: 220 - Carbohydrates: 8g - Protein: 25g - Fat: 9g

Grilled Salmon with Asparagus

Servings: 2   Prep time: 10 min   Cook time: 10 min

INGREDIENTS

- 2 salmon fillets (4-6 ounces each)
- 1 bunch asparagus, trimmed
- 1 tablespoon olive oil
- 1 teaspoon lemon zest
- 1 teaspoon minced garlic
- Salt and pepper to taste
- Lemon wedges for serving

DIRECTIONS

1. Preheat the grill to medium-high heat.
2. Rub the salmon fillets and asparagus with olive oil, lemon zest, minced garlic, salt, and pepper.
3. Place the salmon fillets and asparagus on the grill grates.
4. Grill the salmon for 4-5 minutes per side until it flakes easily with a fork.
5. Grill the asparagus for 5-6 minutes, turning occasionally, until tender and slightly charred.
6. Remove the salmon and asparagus from the grill.
7. Serve the grilled salmon and asparagus with lemon wedges.

Calories: 320 - Carbohydrates: 6g - Protein: 30g - Fat: 20g

Stuffed Bell Peppers

Servings: 4　　　Prep time: 20 min　　　Cook time: 25 min

INGREDIENTS

- 4 bell peppers (any color), tops removed and seeds removed
- 1/2 pound lean ground turkey
- 1/2 cup cooked quinoa
- 1/4 cup diced onion
- 1/4 cup diced zucchini
- 1/4 cup diced mushrooms
- 1/4 cup diced tomatoes
- 1/4 cup grated mozzarella cheese
- 1 teaspoon olive oil
- 1/2 teaspoon dried oregano
- 1/2 teaspoon dried basil
- Salt and pepper to taste

DIRECTIONS

1. Preheat the oven to 375°F (190°C) and prepare a baking dish.
2. In a skillet, heat olive oil over medium heat.
3. Add diced onion, diced zucchini, diced mushrooms, and diced tomatoes to the skillet. Sauté for 5 minutes until vegetables are tender.
4. Add lean ground turkey to the skillet and cook until browned.
5. Stir in cooked quinoa, dried oregano, dried basil, salt, and pepper. Mix well.
6. Stuff each bell pepper with the turkey and quinoa mixture.
7. Place the stuffed bell peppers in the baking dish.
8. Sprinkle grated mozzarella cheese over the top of each bell pepper.
9. Cover the baking dish with foil and bake in the preheated oven for 30 minutes.
10. Remove the foil and bake for an additional 10 minutes until the cheese is melted and bubbly.
11. Let the stuffed bell peppers cool slightly before serving.

Calories: 240 - Carbohydrates: 20g - Protein: 20g - Fat: 8g

Lemon Herb Baked Chicken

Servings: 2　　　Prep time: 10 min　　　Cook time: 25 min

INGREDIENTS

- 2 boneless, skinless chicken breasts
- 1 lemon, juiced and zested
- 2 tablespoons olive oil
- 1 teaspoon dried thyme
- 1 teaspoon dried rosemary
- Salt and pepper to taste

DIRECTIONS

1. Preheat the oven to 400°F (200°C) and prepare a baking dish.
2. In a small bowl, whisk together lemon juice, lemon zest, olive oil, dried thyme, dried rosemary, salt, and pepper.
3. Place the chicken breasts in the baking dish and pour the lemon herb mixture over them.
4. Bake in the preheated oven for 20-25 minutes until the chicken is cooked through and golden brown.
5. Remove from the oven and let the chicken rest for a few minutes before serving.

Calories: 200 - Carbohydrates: 2g - Protein: 30g - Fat: 8g

Shrimp Stir-Fry with Vegetables

Servings: 2 | Prep time: 15 min | Cook time: 10 min

INGREDIENTS

- 1/2 pound shrimp, peeled and deveined
- 1 cup mixed vegetables (such as broccoli florets, bell peppers, snap peas)
- 2 cloves garlic, minced
- 1 tablespoon low-sodium soy sauce
- 1 tablespoon sesame oil
- 1/2 teaspoon grated ginger
- 1/4 teaspoon red pepper flakes (optional)
- Salt and pepper to taste

DIRECTIONS

1. In a large skillet or wok, heat sesame oil over medium heat.
2. Add minced garlic and grated ginger to the skillet and sauté for 1 minute until fragrant.
3. Add shrimp and cook for 2-3 minutes until they turn pink and opaque.
4. Add mixed vegetables to the skillet and stir-fry for 3-4 minutes until they are crisp-tender.
5. In a small bowl, whisk together low-sodium soy sauce and red pepper flakes (if using).
6. Pour the sauce over the shrimp and vegetable mixture in the skillet and toss to coat.
7. Season with salt and pepper to taste.
8. Remove from heat and serve immediately.

Calories: 180 - Carbohydrates: 8g - Protein: 20g - Fat: 6g

Baked Cod with Herbed Quinoa

Servings: 2 | Prep time: 10 min | Cook time: 25 min

INGREDIENTS

- 2 cod fillets (4-6 ounces each)
- 1/2 cup quinoa, rinsed
- 1 cup low-sodium chicken or vegetable broth
- 1 tablespoon chopped fresh parsley
- 1 tablespoon chopped fresh dill
- 1 tablespoon lemon juice
- 1 teaspoon olive oil
- Salt and pepper to taste

DIRECTIONS

1. Preheat the oven to 400°F (200°C) and prepare a baking dish.
2. In a saucepan, bring the broth to a boil. Add rinsed quinoa, reduce heat to low, cover, and simmer for 15 minutes or until the quinoa is cooked and the liquid is absorbed.
3. In a small bowl, mix together chopped parsley, chopped dill, lemon juice, olive oil, salt, and pepper.
4. Place the cod fillets in the baking dish and brush them with the herbed mixture.
5. Bake in the preheated oven for 15-20 minutes until the fish is opaque and flakes easily with a fork.
6. Serve the baked cod over a bed of cooked quinoa.

Calories: 220 - Carbohydrates: 20g - Protein: 25g - Fat: 4g

Shrimp Stir-Fry with Vegetables

Servings: 2   Prep time: 15 min   Cook time: 10 min

INGREDIENTS

- 1/2 pound shrimp, peeled and deveined
- 1 cup mixed vegetables (such as broccoli florets, bell peppers, snap peas)
- 2 cloves garlic, minced
- 1 tablespoon low-sodium soy sauce
- 1 tablespoon sesame oil
- 1/2 teaspoon grated ginger
- 1/4 teaspoon red pepper flakes (optional)
- Salt and pepper to taste

DIRECTIONS

1. In a large skillet or wok, heat sesame oil over medium heat.
2. Add minced garlic and grated ginger to the skillet and sauté for 1 minute until fragrant.
3. Add shrimp and cook for 2-3 minutes until they turn pink and opaque.
4. Add mixed vegetables to the skillet and stir-fry for 3-4 minutes until they are crisp-tender.
5. In a small bowl, whisk together low-sodium soy sauce and red pepper flakes (if using).
6. Pour the sauce over the shrimp and vegetable mixture in the skillet and toss to coat.
7. Season with salt and pepper to taste.
8. Remove from heat and serve immediately.

Calories: 180 - Carbohydrates: 8g - Protein: 20g - Fat: 6g

Baked Cod with Herbed Quinoa

Servings: 2   Prep time: 10 min   Cook time: 25 min

INGREDIENTS

- 2 cod fillets (4-6 ounces each)
- 1/2 cup quinoa, rinsed
- 1 cup low-sodium chicken or vegetable broth
- 1 tablespoon chopped fresh parsley
- 1 tablespoon chopped fresh dill
- 1 tablespoon lemon juice
- 1 teaspoon olive oil
- Salt and pepper to taste

DIRECTIONS

1. Preheat the oven to 400°F (200°C) and prepare a baking dish.
2. In a saucepan, bring the broth to a boil. Add rinsed quinoa, reduce heat to low, cover, and simmer for 15 minutes or until the quinoa is cooked and the liquid is absorbed.
3. In a small bowl, mix together chopped parsley, chopped dill, lemon juice, olive oil, salt, and pepper.
4. Place the cod fillets in the baking dish and brush them with the herbed mixture.
5. Bake in the preheated oven for 15-20 minutes until the fish is opaque and flakes easily with a fork.
6. Serve the baked cod over a bed of cooked quinoa.

Calories: 220 - Carbohydrates: 20g - Protein: 25g - Fat: 4g

Grilled Turkey Burger with Sweet Potato Fries

Servings: 2 Prep time: 15 min Cook time: 20 min

INGREDIENTS

- 8 ounces ground turkey
- 2 whole wheat burger buns
- 2 lettuce leaves
- 2 tomato slices
- 2 red onion slices
- 1 sweet potato, cut into fries
- 1 tablespoon olive oil
- 1/2 teaspoon paprika
- 1/2 teaspoon garlic powder
- Salt and pepper to taste

DIRECTIONS

1. Preheat the grill or stovetop grill pan to medium heat.
2. In a bowl, season ground turkey with salt, pepper, paprika, and garlic powder. Mix well and form two burger patties.
3. Place the turkey burgers on the grill and cook for 4-5 minutes on each side until cooked through.
4. While the burgers are cooking, preheat the oven to 425°F (220°C) and prepare a baking sheet.
5. In a separate bowl, toss the sweet potato fries with olive oil, salt, and pepper.
6. Spread the sweet potato fries in a single layer on the baking sheet and bake for 15-20 minutes until crispy and golden.
7. Toast the burger buns if desired.
8. Assemble the turkey burgers by placing each patty on a bun and topping with lettuce, tomato, and red onion slices.
9. Serve with a side of sweet potato fries.

Calories: 280 - Carbohydrates: 30g - Protein: 25g - Fat: 8g

Baked Eggplant Parmesan

Servings: 2 Prep time: 20 min Cook time: 30 min

INGREDIENTS

- 1 small eggplant, sliced into rounds
- 1/2 cup marinara sauce
- 1/4 cup grated Parmesan cheese
- 1/4 cup shredded mozzarella cheese
- 1/4 cup breadcrumbs
- 1 tablespoon olive oil
- 1 teaspoon dried basil
- 1/2 teaspoon dried oregano
- Salt and pepper to taste

DIRECTIONS

1. Preheat the oven to 400°F (200°C) and prepare a baking sheet.
2. Place the eggplant rounds on the baking sheet and brush both sides with olive oil.
3. In a small bowl, mix together breadcrumbs, dried basil, dried oregano, salt, and pepper.
4. Sprinkle the breadcrumb mixture evenly over the eggplant rounds.
5. Bake in the preheated oven for 15 minutes until the eggplant is tender and the breadcrumbs are golden.
6. Remove from the oven and spoon marinara sauce over each eggplant round.
7. Sprinkle grated Parmesan cheese and shredded mozzarella cheese on top.
8. Return to the oven and bake for another 10-15 minutes until the cheese is melted and bubbly.
9. Serve the baked eggplant Parmesan as a main dish or with a side salad.

Calories: 220 - Carbohydrates: 20g - Protein: 10g - Fat: 10g

Grilled Lemon Herb Chicken with Roasted Vegetables

Servings: 2 Prep time: 15 min Cook time: 25 min

INGREDIENTS

- 2 boneless, skinless chicken breasts
- 1 lemon, juiced and zested
- 2 tablespoons olive oil
- 2 garlic cloves, minced
- 1 teaspoon dried thyme
- 1 teaspoon dried rosemary
- Salt and pepper to taste
- 1 cup mixed vegetables (such as bell peppers, zucchini, and cherry tomatoes), chopped
- Cooking spray

DIRECTIONS

1. Preheat the grill or stovetop grill pan to medium-high heat.
2. In a bowl, combine lemon juice, lemon zest, olive oil, minced garlic, dried thyme, dried rosemary, salt, and pepper.
3. Place the chicken breasts in the bowl and coat them evenly with the marinade.
4. Let the chicken marinate for at least 10 minutes.
5. Meanwhile, preheat the oven to 400°F (200°C) and prepare a baking sheet.
6. Toss the chopped vegetables with olive oil, salt, and pepper.
7. Spread the vegetables in a single layer on the baking sheet.
8. Roast the vegetables in the preheated oven for 20-25 minutes until tender and slightly charred.
9. While the vegetables are roasting, grill the marinated chicken breasts for 6-8 minutes on each side until cooked through.
10. Remove the chicken from the grill and let it rest for a few minutes before slicing.
11. Serve the grilled lemon herb chicken with the roasted vegetables.

Calories: 200 - Carbohydrates: 10g - Protein: 25g - Fat: 8g

Baked Cod with Lemon Herb Crust

Servings: 2 Prep time: 10 min Cook time: 20 min

INGREDIENTS

- 2 cod fillets (4-6 ounces each)
- 2 tablespoons fresh parsley, chopped
- 1 tablespoon fresh dill, chopped
- 1 tablespoon fresh chives, chopped
- 1 tablespoon lemon juice
- 1 tablespoon olive oil
- 1 garlic clove, minced
- Salt and pepper to taste
- Lemon wedges for serving

DIRECTIONS

1. Preheat the oven to 400°F (200°C) and prepare a baking dish.
2. In a small bowl, combine chopped parsley, dill, chives, lemon juice, olive oil, minced garlic, salt, and pepper.
3. Pat the cod fillets dry with a paper towel and place them in the baking dish.
4. Spread the herb mixture evenly over the cod fillets.
5. Bake the cod in the preheated oven for 15-20 minutes until it flakes easily with a fork.
6. Remove the cod from the oven and let it rest for a few minutes.
7. Serve the baked cod with lemon wedges.

Calories: 180 - Carbohydrates: 2g - Protein: 30g - Fat: 6g

Turkey Meatballs with Zucchini Noodles

Servings: 2　　　Prep time: 20 min　　　Cook time: 25 min

INGREDIENTS

- 8 ounces lean ground turkey
- 1/4 cup grated Parmesan cheese
- 1/4 cup almond flour
- 1/4 cup chopped fresh parsley
- 1 garlic clove, minced
- 1 egg, lightly beaten
- Salt and pepper to taste
- 2 zucchini, spiralized into noodles
- 1 cup marinara sauce (look for low-sugar or sugar-free options)
- 1 tablespoon olive oil
- Fresh basil leaves for garnish (optional)

DIRECTIONS

1. Preheat the oven to 375°F (190°C) and line a baking sheet with parchment paper.
2. In a mixing bowl, combine ground turkey, grated Parmesan cheese, almond flour, chopped parsley, minced garlic, beaten egg, salt, and pepper.
3. Mix everything together until well combined.
4. Shape the turkey mixture into small meatballs, approximately 1 inch in diameter.
5. Place the meatballs on the prepared baking sheet and bake them in the preheated oven for 20-25 minutes until cooked through.
6. While the meatballs are baking, heat olive oil in a skillet over medium heat.
7. Add the spiralized zucchini noodles to the skillet and sauté for 2-3 minutes until tender.
8. Pour the marinara sauce over the zucchini noodles and heat it through.
9. Once the meatballs are done, add them to the skillet with the zucchini noodles and sauce.
10. Gently toss everything together to coat the meatballs and noodles with the sauce.
11. Garnish with fresh basil leaves, if desired, and serve the turkey meatballs with zucchini noodles.

Calories: 230 - Carbohydrates: 10g - Protein: 25g - Fat: 10g

Asian-Inspired Beef Stir-Fry

Servings: 2　　　Prep time: 15 min　　　Cook time: 10 min

INGREDIENTS

- 8 ounces lean beef sirloin, thinly sliced
- 1 tablespoon low-sodium soy sauce
- 1 tablespoon rice vinegar
- 1 tablespoon hoisin sauce
- 1 teaspoon sesame oil
- 1 teaspoon cornstarch
- 1/2 cup sliced bell peppers (assorted colors)
- 1/2 cup snap peas
- 1/2 cup sliced mushrooms
- 1/4 cup sliced scallions
- 1 garlic clove, minced
- 1 tablespoon olive oil
- Sesame seeds for garnish (optional)

DIRECTIONS

1. In a small bowl, whisk together low-sodium soy sauce, rice vinegar, hoisin sauce, sesame oil, and cornstarch.
2. Add the sliced beef to the bowl and toss to coat it evenly with the marinade.
3. Let the beef marinate for at least 10 minutes.
4. Heat olive oil in a skillet or wok over medium-high heat.
5. Add minced garlic and sliced scallions to the skillet and sauté for 1-2 minutes until fragrant.
6. Add the marinated beef to the skillet and stir-fry for 2-3 minutes until browned and cooked to your desired doneness.
7. Remove the beef from the skillet and set it aside.
8. In the same skillet, add the sliced bell peppers, snap peas, and mushrooms.
9. Stir-fry the vegetables for 3-4 minutes until crisp-tender.
10. Return the cooked beef to the skillet and pour the remaining marinade over the mixture.
11. Toss everything together and cook for an additional 1-2 minutes to combine the flavors.
12. Garnish with sesame seeds, if desired, and serve the Asian-inspired beef stir-fry.

Calories: 220 - Carbohydrates: 10g - Protein: 25g - Fat: 8g

Stuffed Bell Peppers with Turkey and Quinoa

Servings: 2 Prep time: 20 min Cook time: 45 min

INGREDIENTS

- 2 large bell peppers (assorted colors), tops removed and seeded
- 8 ounces lean ground turkey
- 1/2 cup cooked quinoa
- 1/4 cup chopped onion
- 1/4 cup diced tomatoes
- 2 tablespoons grated Parmesan cheese
- 1 tablespoon chopped fresh parsley
- 1 teaspoon olive oil
- 1 garlic clove, minced
- Salt and pepper to taste

DIRECTIONS

1. Preheat the oven to 375°F (190°C) and prepare a baking dish.
2. Place the bell peppers in the baking dish, standing upright.
3. In a skillet, heat olive oil over medium heat.
4. Add minced garlic and chopped onion to the skillet and sauté for 2-3 minutes until softened.
5. Add the ground turkey to the skillet and cook until browned and cooked through.
6. Remove the skillet from the heat and stir in cooked quinoa, diced tomatoes, grated Parmesan cheese, chopped parsley, salt, and pepper.
7. Spoon the turkey and quinoa mixture into the hollowed-out bell peppers, filling them to the top.
8. Cover the baking dish with foil and bake the stuffed bell peppers in the preheated oven for 35-40 minutes until the peppers are tender.
9. Remove the foil and bake for an additional 5 minutes to lightly brown the tops.
10. Remove the stuffed bell peppers from the oven and let them cool slightly before serving.

Calories: 240 - Carbohydrates: 20g - Protein: 25g - Fat: 8g

Seared Salmon with Quinoa and Steamed Asparagus

Servings: 2 Prep time: 15 min Cook time: 20 min

INGREDIENTS

- 2 salmon fillets (4-6 ounces each)
- 1 cup cooked quinoa
- 1 bunch asparagus, ends trimmed
- 1 lemon, sliced
- 2 tablespoons olive oil
- Salt and pepper to taste

DIRECTIONS

1. Season the salmon fillets with salt and pepper on both sides.
2. Heat olive oil in a skillet over medium-high heat.
3. Add the salmon fillets to the skillet, skin side down.
4. Cook the salmon for 4-5 minutes on each side until it is seared and cooked to your desired doneness.
5. Remove the salmon from the skillet and set it aside.
6. In a steamer basket, steam the asparagus for 4-5 minutes until crisp-tender.
7. Divide the cooked quinoa onto two plates and top it with the seared salmon fillets and steamed asparagus.
8. Squeeze fresh lemon juice over the dish and garnish with lemon slices.
9. Serve the seared salmon with quinoa and steamed asparagus.

Calories: 280 - Carbohydrates: 20g - Protein: 30g - Fat: 12g

Mexican Chicken Lettuce Wraps

Servings: 2   Prep time: 20 min   Cook time: 15 min

INGREDIENTS

- 2 boneless, skinless chicken breasts, cooked and shredded
- 1/2 cup black beans, rinsed and drained
- 1/4 cup diced tomatoes
- 1/4 cup diced red onion
- 1/4 cup chopped fresh cilantro
- 1 jalapeño pepper, seeded and minced
- 1 lime, juiced
- 1 tablespoon olive oil
- 1 teaspoon ground cumin
- Salt and pepper to taste
- 8 large lettuce leaves (such as butter lettuce or romaine)

DIRECTIONS

1. In a mixing bowl, combine shredded chicken, black beans, diced tomatoes, diced red onion, chopped cilantro, minced jalapeño pepper, lime juice, olive oil, ground cumin, salt, and pepper.
2. Toss everything together until well combined and the flavors are incorporated.
3. Place a scoop of the chicken mixture onto each lettuce leaf.
4. Wrap the lettuce leaves around the filling to create lettuce wraps.
5. Secure the wraps with toothpicks if needed.
6. Serve the Mexican chicken lettuce wraps.

Calories: 200 - Carbohydrates: 10g - Protein: 25g - Fat: 6g

Veggie Quinoa Bowl

Servings: 2   Prep time: 15 min   Cook time: 20 min

INGREDIENTS

- 1 cup quinoa
- 2 cups vegetable broth
- 1 tablespoon olive oil
- 1 small onion, diced
- 2 cloves garlic, minced
- 1 bell pepper, diced
- 1 zucchini, diced
- 1 cup cherry tomatoes, halved
- 1 cup cooked chickpeas
- 2 cups fresh spinach
- 1 teaspoon dried oregano
- Salt and pepper to taste
- Fresh lemon juice (optional)

DIRECTIONS

1. Rinse the quinoa under cold water to remove any bitterness. In a saucepan, bring the vegetable broth to a boil. Add the quinoa, reduce heat to low, cover, and simmer for about 15-20 minutes or until all the liquid is absorbed and the quinoa is cooked. Fluff the quinoa with a fork and set aside.
2. In a large skillet, heat the olive oil over medium heat. Add the diced onion and minced garlic, and sauté until they become translucent and fragrant.
3. Add the bell pepper and zucchini to the skillet and cook for about 5 minutes until they start to soften.
4. Stir in the cherry tomatoes, cooked chickpeas, dried oregano, salt, and pepper. Cook for an additional 2-3 minutes.
5. Add the fresh spinach to the skillet and cook until wilted.
6. To assemble the bowl, divide the cooked quinoa among serving bowls. Top with the vegetable mixture from the skillet.
7. Squeeze some fresh lemon juice over the bowl for added brightness, if desired.
8. Give the bowl a gentle toss to combine all the flavors.
9. Serve the Veggie Quinoa Bowl warm and enjoy!

Calories: 350 - Carbohydrates: 55g - Protein: 12g - Fat: 8g

Greek Yogurt Parfait

Servings: 1   Prep time: 5 min   Cook time: /

INGREDIENTS

- 1/2 cup plain Greek yogurt
- 1/4 cup fresh berries (such as strawberries, blueberries, or raspberries)
- 1 tablespoon chopped nuts (such as almonds or walnuts)
- 1 teaspoon honey (optional)

DIRECTIONS

1. In a small bowl or glass, layer the Greek yogurt, fresh berries, and chopped nuts.
2. Drizzle honey on top, if desired.
3. Serve and enjoy!

Calories: 150 - Carbohydrates: 10g - Protein: 12g - Fat: 6g

Caprese Skewers

Servings: 2   Prep time: 10 min   Cook time: /

INGREDIENTS

- 6 cherry tomatoes
- 6 small fresh mozzarella balls
- 6 fresh basil leaves
- 1 tablespoon balsamic glaze

DIRECTIONS

1. Thread one cherry tomato, one mozzarella ball, and one basil leaf onto a small skewer or toothpick.
2. Repeat with the remaining ingredients.
3. Drizzle balsamic glaze over the skewers.
4. Serve and enjoy!

Calories: 120 - Carbohydrates: 6g - Protein: 8g - Fat: 8g

Deviled Eggs

Servings: 4 Prep time: 15 min Cook time: 12 min

INGREDIENTS

- 4 hard-boiled eggs
- 2 tablespoons mayonnaise
- 1 teaspoon Dijon mustard
- 1/2 teaspoon white vinegar
- Salt and pepper to taste
- Paprika for garnish (optional)

DIRECTIONS

1. Cut the hard-boiled eggs in half lengthwise and remove the yolks.
2. In a bowl, mash the egg yolks with mayonnaise, Dijon mustard, white vinegar, salt, and pepper until smooth.
3. Spoon the yolk mixture back into the egg white halves.
4. Sprinkle paprika on top for garnish, if desired.
5. Serve and enjoy!

Calories: 140 - Carbohydrates: 1g - Protein: 7g - Fat: 12g

Cottage Cheese with Fresh Fruit

Servings: 1 Prep time: 10 min Cook time: /

INGREDIENTS

- 1/2 cup low-fat cottage cheese
- 1/2 cup fresh fruit (such as sliced strawberries, blueberries, or peaches)

DIRECTIONS

1. In a bowl, combine the low-fat cottage cheese and fresh fruit.
2. Stir gently to mix.
3. Serve and enjoy!

Calories: 120 - Carbohydrates: 10g - Protein: 15g - Fat: 2g

Roasted Chickpeas

Servings: 4   Prep time: 5 min   Cook time: 25 min

INGREDIENTS

- 1 can (15 ounces) chickpeas (garbanzo beans), drained and rinsed
- 1 tablespoon olive oil
- 1 teaspoon ground cumin
- 1/2 teaspoon smoked paprika
- 1/2 teaspoon garlic powder
- Salt to taste

DIRECTIONS

1. Preheat the oven to 400 °F (200°C) and line a baking sheet with parchment paper.
2. In a bowl, toss the drained and rinsed chickpeas with olive oil, ground cumin, smoked paprika, garlic powder, and salt until well coated.
3. Spread the chickpeas in a single layer on the prepared baking sheet.
4. Roast in the preheated oven for 25 minutes, stirring halfway through, until crispy.
5. Remove from the oven and let cool before serving.

Calories: 150 - Carbohydrates: 20g - Protein: 7g - Fat: 5g

Cottage Cheese with Fresh Fruit

Servings: 1   Prep time: 10 min   Cook time: /

INGREDIENTS

- 1/2 cup low-fat cottage cheese
- 1/2 cup fresh fruit (such as sliced strawberries, blueberries, or peaches)

DIRECTIONS

1. In a bowl, combine the low-fat cottage cheese and fresh fruit.
2. Stir gently to mix.
3. Serve and enjoy!

Calories: 120 - Carbohydrates: 10g - Protein: 15g - Fat: 2g

Turkey Lettuce Wraps

Servings: 2 Prep time: 15 min Cook time: 10 min

INGREDIENTS

- 8 ounces lean ground turkey
- 1/4 cup diced bell peppers (assorted colors)
- 1/4 cup diced zucchini
- 2 tablespoons diced onion
- 1 garlic clove, minced
- 2 tablespoons low-sodium soy sauce
- 1 tablespoon hoisin sauce
- 1 tablespoon olive oil
- 8 large lettuce leaves (such as butter lettuce or romaine)

DIRECTIONS

1. In a skillet, heat olive oil over medium-high heat.
2. Add minced garlic, diced bell peppers, diced zucchini, and diced onion to the skillet.
3. Sauté for 3-4 minutes until the vegetables are softened.
4. Add the ground turkey to the skillet and cook until browned and cooked through.
5. Stir in low-sodium soy sauce and hoisin sauce, and cook for an additional 2 minutes to combine the flavors.
6. Divide the turkey mixture onto the lettuce leaves.
7. Roll up the lettuce leaves to create wraps.
8. Serve and enjoy!

Calories: 180 - Carbohydrates: 8g - Protein: 20g - Fat: 8g

Tuna Cucumber Bites

Servings: 2 Prep time: 10 min Cook time: /

INGREDIENTS

- 1 can (5 ounces) tuna in water, drained
- 2 tablespoons Greek yogurt
- 1 tablespoon chopped fresh dill
- 1 tablespoon diced red onion
- 1 cucumber, sliced into rounds

DIRECTIONS

1. In a bowl, combine drained tuna, Greek yogurt, chopped fresh dill, and diced red onion.
2. Stir until well mixed.
3. Place a spoonful of the tuna mixture on each cucumber round.
4. Serve and enjoy!

Calories: 100 - Carbohydrates: 4g - Protein: 15g - Fat: 2g

Veggie Egg Muffins

Servings: 4   Prep time: 15 min   Cook time: 20 min

INGREDIENTS

- 4 large eggs
- 1/4 cup diced bell peppers (assorted colors)
- 1/4 cup diced zucchini
- 1/4 cup diced mushrooms
- 2 tablespoons diced onion
- 2 tablespoons shredded cheddar cheese
- Salt and pepper to taste

DIRECTIONS

1. Preheat the oven to 375°F (190°C) and grease a muffin tin with cooking spray.
2. In a bowl, whisk the eggs together.
3. Stir in diced bell peppers, diced zucchini, diced mushrooms, diced onion, shredded cheddar cheese, salt, and pepper.
4. Pour the egg mixture evenly into the greased muffin tin.
5. Bake in the preheated oven for 18-20 minutes until the muffins are set and golden.
6. Remove from the oven and let cool slightly before serving.

Calories: 120 - Carbohydrates: 4g - Protein: 10g - Fat: 6g

Apple Slices with Almond Butter

Servings: 1   Prep time: 10 min   Cook time: /

INGREDIENTS

- 1 apple, sliced
- 1 tablespoon almond butter

DIRECTIONS

1. Dip apple slices into almond butter.
2. Serve and enjoy!

Calories: 150 - Carbohydrates: 20g - Protein: 4g - Fat: 8g

Protein Shake

Servings: 1 Prep time: 5 min Cook time: 20 min

INGREDIENTS

- 1 cup unsweetened almond milk
- 1 scoop protein powder (vanilla or chocolate flavor)
- 1/2 frozen banana
- 1 tablespoon almond butter

DIRECTIONS

1. In a blender, combine unsweetened almond milk, protein powder, frozen banana, and almond butter.
2. Blend until smooth and creamy.
3. Serve and enjoy!

Calories: 250 - Carbohydrates: 15g - Protein: 25g - Fat: 10g

Apple Slices with Almond Butter

Servings: 1 Prep time: 10 min Cook time: /

INGREDIENTS

- 1 apple, sliced
- 1 tablespoon almond butter

DIRECTIONS

1. Dip apple slices into almond butter.
2. Serve and enjoy!

Calories: 150 - Carbohydrates: 20g - Protein: 4g - Fat: 8g

Smoothies

Berry Blast Smoothie

Servings: 1 Prep time: 5 min Cook time: /

INGREDIENTS

- 1/2 cup frozen mixed berries
- 1/2 cup unsweetened almond milk
- 1/4 cup Greek yogurt
- 1 tablespoon chia seeds
- 1 tablespoon honey (optional)

DIRECTIONS

1. Place all the ingredients in a blender.
2. Blend until smooth and creamy.
3. Pour into a glass and enjoy!

Calories: 150 - Carbohydrates: 20g - Protein: 7g - Fat: 4g

Green Detox Smoothie

Servings: 1 Prep time: 5 min Cook time: /

INGREDIENTS

- 1 cup fresh spinach
- 1/2 small cucumber
- 1/2 green apple
- 1/4 cup fresh parsley
- 1/4 avocado
- 1/2 cup coconut water
- Juice of 1/2 lemon

DIRECTIONS

1. Add all the ingredients to a blender.
2. Blend until smooth and well combined.
3. Pour into a glass and enjoy!

Calories: 120 - Carbohydrates: 14g - Protein: 4g - Fat: 6g

Tropical Paradise Smoothie

Servings: 1 Prep time: 5 min Cook time: /

INGREDIENTS

- 1/2 cup frozen pineapple chunks
- 1/2 cup frozen mango chunks
- 1/4 cup coconut milk
- 1/4 cup Greek yogurt
- 1 tablespoon shredded coconut (optional)
- 1 tablespoon flaxseeds

DIRECTIONS

1. Place all the ingredients in a blender.
2. Blend until smooth and creamy.
3. Pour into a glass and enjoy!

Calories: 150 - Carbohydrates: 20g - Protein: 7g - Fat: 4g

Green Detox Smoothie

Servings: 1 Prep time: 5 min Cook time: /

INGREDIENTS

- 1 cup fresh spinach
- 1/2 small cucumber
- 1/2 green apple
- 1/4 cup fresh parsley
- 1/4 avocado
- 1/2 cup coconut water
- Juice of 1/2 lemon

DIRECTIONS

1. Add all the ingredients to a blender.
2. Blend until smooth and well combined.
3. Pour into a glass and enjoy!

Calories: 160 - Carbohydrates: 25g - Protein: 7g - Fat: 5g

Peanut Butter Banana Smoothie

Servings: 1 Prep time: 5 min Cook time: /

INGREDIENTS

- 1 ripe banana
- 1 tablespoon natural peanut butter
- 1 cup unsweetened almond milk
- 1/4 cup Greek yogurt
- 1 tablespoon honey (optional)
- Ice cubes (optional)

DIRECTIONS

1. In a blender, combine the ripe banana, peanut butter, almond milk, Greek yogurt, and honey.
2. Blend until smooth and creamy.
3. Add ice cubes if desired and blend again.
4. Pour into a glass and enjoy!

Calories: 210 - Carbohydrates: 25g - Protein: 9g - Fat: 9g

Creamy Berry Avocado Smoothie

Servings: 1 Prep time: 5 min Cook time: /

INGREDIENTS

- 1/2 cup frozen mixed berries
- 1/4 ripe avocado
- 1/2 cup unsweetened almond milk
- 1/4 cup Greek yogurt
- 1 tablespoon honey (optional)

DIRECTIONS

1. Place all the ingredients in a blender.
2. Blend until smooth and creamy.
3. Pour into a glass and enjoy!

Calories: 180 - Carbohydrates: 22g - Protein: 8g - Fat: 7g

Chocolate Banana Protein Smoothie

Servings: 1   Prep time: 5 min   Cook time: /

INGREDIENTS

- 1 ripe banana
- 1 scoop chocolate protein powder
- 1 cup unsweetened almond milk
- 1 tablespoon almond butter
- Ice cubes (optional)

DIRECTIONS

1. In a blender, combine the ripe banana, chocolate protein powder, almond milk, and almond butter.
2. Blend until smooth and well combined.
3. Add ice cubes if desired and blend again.
4. Pour into a glass and enjoy!

Calories: 250 - Carbohydrates: 25g - Protein: 25g - Fat: 10g

Spinach and Mango Smoothie

Servings: 1   Prep time: 5 min   Cook time: /

INGREDIENTS

- 1 cup fresh spinach
- 1/2 cup frozen mango chunks
- 1/4 cup Greek yogurt
- 1/2 cup unsweetened almond milk
- 1 tablespoon chia seeds

DIRECTIONS

1. Add all the ingredients to a blender.
2. Blend until smooth and well combined.
3. Pour into a glass and enjoy!

Calories: 130 - Carbohydrates: 18g - Protein: 7g - Fat: 4g

Raspberry Almond Smoothie

Servings: 1 Prep time: 5 min Cook time: /

INGREDIENTS

- 1/2 cup frozen raspberries
- 1/4 cup almond milk
- 1/4 cup Greek yogurt
- 1 tablespoon almond butter
- 1 tablespoon flaxseeds

DIRECTIONS

1. Place all the ingredients in a blender.
2. Blend until smooth and creamy.
3. Pour into a glass and enjoy!

Calories: 140 - Carbohydrates: 15g - Protein: 6g - Fat: 7g

Peach Oatmeal Smoothie

Servings: 1 Prep time: 5 min Cook time: /

INGREDIENTS

- 1/2 cup frozen peaches
- 1/4 cup rolled oats
- 1/2 cup unsweetened almond milk
- 1/4 cup Greek yogurt
- 1 tablespoon honey (optional)
- 1/2 teaspoon vanilla extract

DIRECTIONS

1. Add all the ingredients to a blender.
2. Blend until smooth and creamy.
3. Pour into a glass and enjoy!

Calories: 180 - Carbohydrates: 25g - Protein: 8g - Fat: 4g

Coconut Pineapple Smoothie

Servings: 1　　　　Prep time: 5 min　　　　Cook time: /

INGREDIENTS

- 1/2 cup frozen pineapple chunks
- 1/2 cup coconut milk
- 1/4 cup Greek yogurt
- 1 tablespoon shredded coconut (optional)

DIRECTIONS

1. Place all the ingredients in a blender.
2. Blend until smooth and creamy.
3. Pour into a glass and enjoy!

Calories: 170 - Carbohydrates: 20g - Protein: 6g - Fat: 9g

Sweet

Berry Chia Pudding

Servings: 2 | Prep time: 10 min | Cook time: /

INGREDIENTS

- 1 cup unsweetened almond milk
- 2 tablespoons chia seeds
- 1 tablespoon honey or a sugar substitute
- 1/2 teaspoon vanilla extract
- 1/2 cup mixed berries (strawberries, blueberries, raspberries)

DIRECTIONS

1. In a bowl, combine the almond milk, chia seeds, honey or sugar substitute, and vanilla extract. Stir well.
2. Let the mixture sit for 10 minutes, stirring occasionally to prevent clumping.
3. Refrigerate for at least 2 hours or overnight until the mixture thickens and forms a pudding-like consistency.
4. Serve in individual bowls or glasses and top with mixed berries.

Calories: 120 - Carbohydrates: 12g - Protein: 3g - Fat: 6g

Baked Apples with Cinnamon

Servings: 2 | Prep time: 5 min | Cook time: 25 min

INGREDIENTS

- 2 small apples (such as Granny Smith or Honeycrisp)
- 1 tablespoon melted coconut oil
- 1 tablespoon honey or a sugar substitute
- 1 teaspoon ground cinnamon

DIRECTIONS

1. Preheat the oven to 375°F (190°C).
2. Core the apples using an apple corer or a knife, leaving the bottoms intact.
3. In a small bowl, mix together the melted coconut oil, honey or sugar substitute, and cinnamon.
4. Place the apples in a baking dish and brush the cinnamon mixture over each apple, ensuring they are well coated.
5. Bake in the preheated oven for about 25 minutes or until the apples are tender.
6. Serve warm as is or with a dollop of Greek yogurt if desired.

Calories: 150 - Carbohydrates: 25g - Protein: 1g - Fat: 6g

Greek Yogurt Parfait

Servings: 1 Prep time: 10 min Cook time: /

INGREDIENTS

- 1/2 cup non-fat Greek yogurt
- 1/4 cup fresh berries (strawberries, blueberries, raspberries)
- 1 tablespoon chopped nuts (such as almonds or walnuts)
- 1 tablespoon unsweetened shredded coconut
- 1 teaspoon honey or a sugar substitute

DIRECTIONS

1. In a glass or bowl, layer the Greek yogurt, fresh berries, chopped nuts, and shredded coconut.
2. Drizzle with honey or sprinkle with a sugar substitute.
3. Repeat the layers until all the ingredients are used.
4. Serve immediately.

Calories: 180 - Carbohydrates: 16g - Protein: 18g - Fat: 7g

Banana-Oat Cookies

Servings: 6 Prep time: 15 min Cook time: 15 min

INGREDIENTS

- 2 ripe bananas, mashed
- 1 cup old-fashioned oats
- 2 tablespoons almond butter
- 1/4 teaspoon ground cinnamon
- 1/4 teaspoon vanilla extract
- 2 tablespoons dark chocolate chips (optional)

DIRECTIONS

1. Preheat the oven to 350°F (175°C) and line a baking sheet with parchment paper.
2. In a bowl, combine the mashed bananas, oats, almond butter, cinnamon, vanilla extract, and dark chocolate chips (if using).
3. Stir until all the ingredients are well combined.
4. Drop spoonfuls of the mixture onto the prepared baking sheet and flatten them slightly with the back of a spoon.
5. Bake in the preheated oven for about 15 minutes or until the cookies are lightly golden.
6. Allow the cookies to cool on the baking sheet for a few minutes before transferring them to a wire rack to cool completely.

Calories: 130 - Carbohydrates: 21g - Protein: 3g - Fat: 4g

Strawberry Banana Nice Cream

Servings: 2   Prep time: 5 min   Cook time: /

INGREDIENTS

- 2 ripe bananas, sliced and frozen
- 1 cup frozen strawberries
- 1/4 cup unsweetened almond milk or coconut milk

DIRECTIONS

1. Place the frozen banana slices, frozen strawberries, and almond milk or coconut milk in a blender or food processor.
2. Blend until smooth and creamy, scraping down the sides as needed.
3. If the mixture is too thick, add more almond milk or coconut milk as necessary.
4. Serve immediately as soft-serve ice cream or transfer to a container and freeze for a firmer texture.

Calories: 110 - Carbohydrates: 27g - Protein: 1g - Fat: 1g

Lemon Poppy Seed Muffins

Servings: 6   Prep time: 15 min   Cook time: 20 min

INGREDIENTS

- 1 cup almond flour
- 2 tablespoons coconut flour
- 1/4 cup sugar substitute
- 1 teaspoon baking powder
- 1 tablespoon poppy seeds
- 1/4 teaspoon salt
- 1/4 cup unsweetened almond milk
- 2 tablespoons lemon juice
- 2 tablespoons melted coconut oil
- 1 teaspoon vanilla extract
- Zest of 1 lemon
- 2 eggs

DIRECTIONS

1. Preheat the oven to 350°F (175°C) and line a muffin tin with paper liners.
2. In a bowl, whisk together the almond flour, coconut flour, sugar substitute, baking powder, poppy seeds, and salt.
3. In another bowl, whisk together the almond milk, lemon juice, melted coconut oil, vanilla extract, lemon zest, and eggs.
4. Pour the wet ingredients into the dry ingredients and stir until just combined.
5. Divide the batter among the prepared muffin cups, filling them about three-fourths full.
6. Bake in the preheated oven for approximately 20 minutes or until a toothpick inserted into the center of a muffin comes out clean.
7. Allow the muffins to cool in the tin for a few minutes before transferring them to a wire rack to cool completely.

Calories: 170 - Carbohydrates: 6g - Protein: 6g - Fat: 14g

Cinnamon Apple Crisp

Servings: 4 Prep time: 15 min Cook time: 30 min

INGREDIENTS

- 2 medium apples, peeled, cored, and sliced
- 1 tablespoon lemon juice
- 1/2 teaspoon ground cinnamon
- 1/4 cup almond flour
- 1/4 cup rolled oats
- 1 tablespoon coconut oil, melted
- 1 tablespoon honey or a sugar substitute

DIRECTIONS

1. Preheat the oven to 350°F (175°C) and lightly grease a baking dish.
2. In a bowl, toss the apple slices with lemon juice and ground cinnamon.
3. Transfer the apple mixture to the prepared baking dish and spread it evenly.
4. In a separate bowl, combine the almond flour, rolled oats, melted coconut oil, and honey or sugar substitute. Mix well until the mixture resembles coarse crumbs.
5. Sprinkle the crumb mixture over the apples in the baking dish.
6. Bake in the preheated oven for about 30 minutes or until the apples are tender and the topping is golden brown.
7. Serve warm and enjoy!

Calories: 130 - Carbohydrates: 20g - Protein: 2g - Fat: 6g

Protein Pancakes

Servings: 2 Prep time: 10 min Cook time: 10 min

INGREDIENTS

- 1/2 cup rolled oats
- 1/2 cup cottage cheese
- 2 eggs
- 1 tablespoon almond flour
- 1/2 teaspoon baking powder
- 1/2 teaspoon vanilla extract
- 1/4 teaspoon cinnamon

DIRECTIONS

1. Place the rolled oats, cottage cheese, eggs, almond flour, baking powder, vanilla extract, and cinnamon in a blender or food processor.
2. Blend until the mixture is smooth and well combined.
3. Preheat a non-stick skillet or griddle over medium heat.
4. Pour approximately 1/4 cup of the batter onto the skillet for each pancake.
5. Cook until bubbles form on the surface of the pancake, then flip and cook for another minute or until golden brown.
6. Repeat with the remaining batter.
7. Serve the pancakes with your choice of toppings, such as fresh berries or a drizzle of sugar-free syrup.

Calories: 220 - Carbohydrates: 18g - Protein: 19g - Fat: 8g

Chocolate Banana Protein Bites

Servings: 10 | Prep time: 15 min | Cook time: /

INGREDIENTS

- 1 ripe banana, mashed
- 1/4 cup almond butter
- 1/4 cup unsweetened cocoa powder
- 1/4 cup protein powder (vanilla or chocolate flavor)
- 1 tablespoon honey or a sugar substitute
- 1/4 cup chopped almonds (optional)

DIRECTIONS

1. In a bowl, combine the mashed banana, almond butter, cocoa powder, protein powder, and honey or sugar substitute. Mix well until all the ingredients are thoroughly combined.
2. If desired, fold in the chopped almonds for added crunch.
3. Roll the mixture into bite-sized balls and place them on a baking sheet lined with parchment paper.
4. Refrigerate for at least 30 minutes to allow the bites to firm up.
5. Store in an airtight container in the refrigerator until ready to enjoy.

Calories: 70 - Carbohydrates: 5g - Protein: 4g - Fat: 4g

Vanilla Almond Pudding

Servings: 2 | Prep time: 10 min | Cook time: /

INGREDIENTS

- 1 cup unsweetened almond milk
- 2 tablespoons almond flour
- 1 tablespoon sugar substitute
- 1/2 teaspoon vanilla extract
- Sliced almonds

DIRECTIONS

1. In a saucepan, whisk together the almond milk, almond flour, sugar substitute, and vanilla extract.
2. Cook over medium heat, stirring constantly, until the mixture thickens to a pudding-like consistency.
3. Remove from heat and let the pudding cool for a few minutes.
4. Transfer the pudding to individual serving dishes and refrigerate for at least 1 hour or until chilled and set.
5. Before serving, garnish with sliced almonds if desired.

Calories: 80 - Carbohydrates: 4g - Protein: 3g - Fat: 6g

Hi, I'm Robert

12/11/1972
Zodiac Sign Scorpio
Height, 181 cm

Who am I ?

Robert is a journalist passionate about nutrition, diet, and exercise. From a young age, he has shown a keen interest in health and wellness, recognizing the importance of a balanced diet and an active lifestyle.

After obtaining a degree in journalism, Robert decided to specialize in the field of nutrition and fitness. He began studying various dietary theories and exploring the most effective approaches to maintaining a healthy lifestyle. During his educational journey, he learned the fundamentals of food science and developed a deep understanding of how food affects the body and mind.

With a solid knowledge base, Robert started writing articles on diets, nutrition, and training for various magazines and websites. He worked with industry experts and interviewed renowned nutritionists, dieticians, and personal trainers to gain a broader perspective on best practices in this field.

Robert's mission is to educate the public about adopting a healthy approach to nutrition and exercise. He believes that good nutrition is essential for achieving a balanced life and that regular physical activity is crucial for long-term well-being.

In addition to writing informative articles, Robert conducts in-depth research on diets and emerging food trends. He constantly seeks to stay updated on the latest scientific discoveries in the field of nutrition and exercise, in order to provide accurate, evidence-based information to his readers.

Robert's passion for nutrition and fitness extends to his personal life as well. He follows a balanced diet and regularly engages in physical activities to maintain fitness and overall well-being. He firmly believes that adopting a healthy lifestyle is an investment in one's future, bringing benefits not only physically but also mentally and emotionally.

Through his work, Robert aims to inspire others to take care of their health through mindful food choices and adequate physical activity. His hope is that the information he shares can help people improve their lives and achieve long-term wellness.

HEALTHY EATING

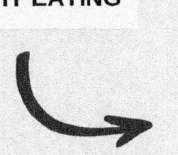

TAKE REGULAR EXERCISE

GOOD RELATIONSHIPS

LIVE BETTER AND LONGER

MEAL PLAN

This is a 4-week meal plan provided for general guidance. Individuals are encouraged to personalize it according to their specific needs and preferences. It is not a one-size-fits-all approach, and users should consider consulting with a healthcare professional or a registered dietitian for personalized advice based on their unique circumstances.

TAKE THE BONUS!

1

High-Intensity Interval Training (HIIT) is a powerful and efficient workout method that has gained tremendous popularity. In just a short duration, HIIT workouts deliver maximum benefits by alternating intense bursts of exercise with short recovery periods. This dynamic approach not only boosts cardiovascular fitness but also accelerates fat burning and enhances muscle tone. With its versatility, HIIT can be adapted to various fitness levels and preferences, making it accessible to a wide range of individuals. Whether it's through bodyweight exercises, cardio routines, or circuit training, HIIT offers a time-efficient and effective way to achieve remarkable fitness results.

This is a 4-week meal plan provided for general guidance. Individuals are encouraged to personalize it according to their specific needs and preferences. It is not a one-size-fits-all approach, and users should consider consulting with a healthcare professional or a registered dietitian for personalized advice based on their unique circumstances.

TAKE THE BONUS! 3

A weight loss journal is a personal diary or log that individuals use to track and document their weight loss journey. It serves as a valuable tool for recording and monitoring various aspects related to weight loss, such as food intake, exercise routines, emotions, and progress. By keeping a weight loss journal, individuals can gain insights into their eating habits, identify patterns, and make informed decisions to support their weight loss goals. It allows for self-reflection, accountability, and the ability to track progress over time, making it an effective tool for promoting and maintaining a healthy lifestyle.

TAKE THE BONUS!

The low FODMAP diet is a dietary approach that involves restricting or minimizing the consumption of certain types of carbohydrates called FODMAPs (Fermentable Oligosaccharides, Disaccharides, Monosaccharides, and Polyols). FODMAPs are known to trigger digestive symptoms in some individuals, particularly those with irritable bowel syndrome (IBS). The diet aims to reduce these symptoms by limiting the intake of foods high in FODMAPs, such as certain fruits, vegetables, grains, dairy products, and sweeteners. It is typically followed under the guidance of a healthcare professional or a registered dietitian.

This book covers the FODMAP diet is a bestseller and is offered as a complimentary gift exclusively to those who purchase this book!

Notes

Notes

Printed in Great Britain
by Amazon